NEVADA WILDLIFE VIEWING GUIDE

Jeanne L. Clark

Helena, Montana

ACKNOWLEDGMENTS

Special thanks for advisory assistance to all of the Nevada Watchable Wildlife Project committee members: Dan Rathbun and JoLynn Worley, Bureau of Land Management; Larry Jones, Department of the Navy; Brenda Hughes, Nevada Department of Tourism; Jenny Neil, Nevada Department of Transportation; Gary Herron and Kim Toulouse, Nevada Department of Wildlife; Barry Whitehill and Anne Janik, US Fish and Wildlife Service; and Steve Anderson and Ron Burraychak, USDA Forest Service.

Warm thanks are also due to the dozens of biologists, on-site managers, and others, who provided nominations, interviews, tours, and text reviews.

Finally, a special thank-you is extended to the Nevada Department of Transportation for providing all of the binocular and directional signing for the project, and to the many federal, state, county, and city agencies that have also joined as partners in signing the viewing network.

State Project Manager: Jim Cole, USDA Forest Service
Author: Jeanne L. Clark
National Watchable Wildlife
Program Coordinator: Kate Davies, Defenders of Wildlife
Illustrations: Clark Ostergaard
Front Cover Photo: *Badger,* MICHAEL S. SAMPLE
Back Cover Photos: *White pelican with chick,* JIM STAMATES
Ruby Mountains, JACK WILBURN

Design, typesetting, and other prepress work by Falcon Press Helena, Montana.

Printed in the United States of America.
ISBN 1-56044-207-7

Cataloging-in-Publication Data
Clark, Jeanne L.
    Nevada wildlife viewing guide / Jeanne L. Clark.
        p. cm. -- (The Watchable Wildlife series)
    Includes index.
    ISBN 1-56044-207-7
    1. Wildlife viewing sites -- Nevada -- Guidebooks. /2. Wildlife watching -- Nevada -- Guidebooks. I. Title. II. Series.
QL 191.C58   1993
599.09793—dc20   93-17494
                                                  CIP

CONTENTS

Project Sponsors 5

Governor's Letter 7

Introduction 8

The National Watchable Wildlife Program 9

The Great Basin Desert 10

Viewing Ethics 12

How to Use this Guide 13

State Map 15

REGION ONE: RENO TAHOE TERRITORY

Regional Map 16

Site 1   Sheldon National Wildlife Refuge 17

Site 2   High Rock Canyon 18

Site 3   Anaho Island National Wildlife Refuge - Pyramid Lake 19

Site 4   Rock Park Trail 20

Site 5   Oxbow Nature Study Area 21

Site 6   Galena Creek Park 22

Site 7   Lake Tahoe State Park 23

Site 8   Jacks Valley Road 24

Site 9   East Fork Carson River 25

REGION TWO: COWBOY COUNTRY

Regional Map 26

Site 10   Lovelock Valley 27

Site 11   Mahogany Creek 28

Site 12   Pine Forest Mountains 29

Great Basin Landscapes: The Playa 30

Site 13   McGill Canyon 32

Site 14   Santa Rosa Mountains 33

Site 15   Summit Trail 34

Site 16   Sonoma Creek 35

Site 17   Wildhorse Crossing Campground 36

Site 18   Bruneau Meadows 37

Site 19   Bear Creek Summit 38

Site 20   Jarbidge Canyon 39

Site 21   Biroth Ridge 40

Site 22   Cabin Field 42

Great Basin Landscapes: The Subalpine Zone 44

Site 23   Angel Lake 43

Site 24   Lamoille Canyon National Scenic Byway 46

Site 25   Ruby Crest National Recreational Trail 47

Site 26   Ruby Lake National Wildlife Refuge 48

Site 27   Goshute Mountains 50

REGION THREE: PONY EXPRESS TERRITORY

Regional Map 51
Site 28   Lahontan State Recreation Area 52
Site 29   Carson Lake 53
Site 30   Stillwater National Wildlife Refuge 54
Site 31   Big Den Creek 55
Site 32   Kingston Canyon 56
Site 33   Steptoe Valley 57
Site 34   Ely Elk Viewing Site 58
Site 35   Success Summit 59
Great Basin Landscapes: The Riparian Zone 60
Site 36   Great Basin National Park 62
Site 37   Cleve Creek 64

REGION FOUR: PIONEER TERRITORY

Regional Map 65
Site 38   Mason Valley Wildlife Management Area 66
Site 39   Wellington Deer Range 67
Site 40   Wilson Canyon 68
Site 41   Walker Lake 69
Site 42   Stewart Creek 70
Site 43   Table Mountain Wilderness 71
Site 44   Chimney Springs 72
Site 45   White River Valley 73
Site 46   Beaver Dam State Park 74
Site 47   Pahranagat National Wildlife Refuge 75
Site 48   Ash Meadows National Wildlife Refuge 76

REGION FIVE: LAS VEGAS TERRITORY

Regional Map 78
Site 49   Bonanza Trailhead 79
Site 50   Mount Charleston Loop 80
Site 51   Corn Creek - Desert National Wildlife Refuge 82
Site 52   Red Rock Canyon National Conservation Area 83
Site 53   Black Canyon 84
Site 54   Virgin River Confluence 85
Site 55   Valley of Fire State Park 86

Wildlife Index 87

PROJECT SPONSORS

THE USDA FOREST SERVICE manages the Toiyabe and Humboldt national forests in Nevada, which encompass more than 5.8 million acres. The USDA Forest Service's mission is to manage resources to benefit the public while protecting these resources for the future. The Eyes on Wildlife program enhances opportunities for all people to experience wildlife, fish, and plant resources and encourages the public to support conservation efforts. USDA Forest Service, 324 25th Street, Ogden, UT, 84401 (801) 625-5347.

THE NEVADA DEPARTMENT OF WILDLIFE—the state's wildlife authority—preserves, protects, manages, and restores wildlife and its habitat within Nevada. The Department's role as protector of the wildlife resource includes managing for all uses, thus creating aesthetic, scientific, educational, recreational, and economic benefits for all people of the state. It's support of the Watchable Wildlife program is a means of recognizing the diverse public interests in Nevada's wildlife resources and the increasing awareness of, concern for, and support of wildlife values and conservation programs. Nevada Department of Wildlife, 1100 Valley Road, Reno, NV 89520 (702) 688-1500.

THE BUREAU OF LAND MANAGEMENT cares for nearly forty-eight million acres in Nevada, roughly sixty-nine percent of the state. As the nation's largest conservation agency, the Bureau of Land Management is dedicated to providing quality habitat to ensure a natural abundance of fish, wildlife, and plants on public lands. The Bureau of Land Management manages the many resources on the public lands—minerals, range, cultural sites, wild horses and burros, wilderness, recreation, and more—under the principles of multiple-use and sustained yield, and within a framework of environmental responsibility. Bureau of Land Management, 850 Harvard Way, Reno, NV 89502 (702) 785-6400.

National Fish and
Wildlife Foundation

THE NATIONAL FISH AND WILDLIFE FOUNDATION, chartered by Congress to stimulate private giving to conservation, is an independent not-for-profit organization. Using federally-funded challenge grants, it forges partnerships between the public and private sectors to conserve the nation's fish, wildlife, and plants. National Fish and Wildlife Foundation, 1120 Connecticut Ave., NW, Washington, DC 20036. (202) 857-0166.

THE NEVADA DEPARTMENT OF TRANSPORTATION is responsible for maintaining approximately 5,430 miles of Nevada's state highways. The Department provides the driving public with a comprehensive, energy-efficient, multi-modal transportation system consistent with social, economic, and environmental objectives. Their general transportation plan provides statistics and maps related to mileage, traffic, and condition of all transportation systems. This plan is used to establish management practices for the construction, operation, and maintenance of roads and highways. District offices are located in Elko, Las Vegas, and Reno. Nevada Department of Transportation, 1263 South Stewart Street, Carson City, NV 89712 (702) 687-4219.

THE US FISH AND WILDLIFE SERVICE administers nearly two million acres of land and water in Nevada, including nine national wildlife refuges, one wildlife management area, and one fish hatchery. The mission of the US Fish and Wildlife Service is to conserve, protect, and enhance fish and wildlife and their habitats for the continuing benefit of the American people. Programs include the National Wildlife Refuge System, protection of threatened and endangered species, conservation of migratory birds, fisheries restoration, recreation/education, wildlife research, and law enforcement. US Fish and Wildlife Service, 911 NE 11th Avenue, Portland, OR 97232 (503) 231-6214.

DEFENDERS OF WILDLIFE is a national nonprofit organization of more than 80,000 members dedicated to preserving the natural abundance and diversity of wildlife and its habitat. A one-year membership is $20 and includes subscriptions to *Defenders*, an award-winning conservation magazine, and *Wildlife Advocate*, an activist-oriented newsletter. To join, or for further information, write or call Defenders of Wildlife, 1244 Nineteenth Street, NW, Washington, D.C. 20036, (202) 659-9510.

THE DEPARTMENT OF DEFENSE is the steward of about twenty-five million acres of land in the United States; many areas possess irreplaceable natural and cultural resources. The Department of Defense supports the Watchable Wildlife Program through its Legacy Resource Management Program, a special initiative to enhance the conservation and restoration of natural and cultural resources on military land. For more information contact the Office of the Deputy Assistant Secretary of Defense (Environment), 400 Army Navy Drive, Suite 206, Arlington, VA 22202-2884.

OTHER IMPORTANT CONTRIBUTORS include Nevada Department of Tourism, Nevada Division of State Parks, National Park Service, Pyramid Lake Paiute Tribe, City of Reno, City of Sparks, Washoe County Parks, Truckee Carson Irrigation District, and the Bureau of Reclamation.

Autumn in Nevada's high desert country brings opportunities for bird watching, solitude, and beauty.
FRED PFLUGHOFT

STATE OF NEVADA
EXECUTIVE CHAMBER
Capitol Complex
Carson City, Nevada 89710

BOB MILLER
Governor

TELEPHONE
(702) 687-5670
Fax: (702) 687-4486

As Governor of Nevada, I am pleased to introduce you to the wonders of Nevada's wildlife heritage.

While Nevada is probably best known for the glamorous excitement of its 24-hour cities, there is another side of the Silver State to discover. Nevada is the driest state in the union, but it is also topographically diverse, with elevations ranging from 500 feet above sea level in the southern deserts to mountains exceeding 13,000 feet. Nevada has a rich diversity of fish and wildlife with over 680 species occurring on our varied landscapes.

Nevada is well known for its quality hunting opportunities, but the state also offers a largely undiscovered opportunity to observe and photograph wildlife in their natural habitats.

A partnership of federal and state agencies, in concert with conservation organizations, has developed this wildlife viewing guide. I invite you to use this viewing guide to assist you in your enjoyment of Nevada's wildlife. Fifty-five viewing sites throughout the state are identified in the guide, and they are marked with special highway signs at each location.

Please accept this invitation to enjoy the other Nevada, its great outdoors and wonderful wildlife.

Sincerely

BOB MILLER
Governor

INTRODUCTION

From rugged mountain peaks bounded by sapphire lakes to teeming wetlands and sprawling desert basins, Nevada provides richly for wildlife. Nevada, the most arid state in the nation, has more diversity in topography than most other states, with elevations ranging from the 470-foot Colorado River border to 13,140-foot Boundary Peak.

This broad range of elevations supports a large and changing array of plant and wildlife species—including more than 370 bird species, 129 mammal species, and 64 reptile and amphibian species. Nevada's seventy million acres include 2,760 miles of streams and 44,000 acres of reservoirs, which provide crucial habitat for nearly 120 species of fish and tens of thousands of migratory birds.

Nevada is a state with many distinctions. The variety of wildlife is impressive, from feather-light swallowtail butterflies to massive Rocky Mountain elk, from desert tortoises to darting Devil's Hole pupfish. Also, Nevada:

- is the nation's most mountainous state, with more than 150 mountain ranges.
- is the driest state, with many areas receiving less than ten inches of precipitation annually.
- has the largest percentage of federal land (85%) in the continental United States.
- sustains the largest number of threatened and endangered fish species.
- supports one of the country's three largest nesting colonies of white-faced ibises at Carson Lake.
- sustains the nation's largest nesting colony of white pelicans at Anaho Island.
- boasts the largest cutthroat trout ever caught, over forty-one pounds.

Nevada's human population is continually expanding. Most of the more than one million residents live in Reno or Las Vegas, distinguishing Nevada as one of the nation's most urban populations. There are excellent wildlife viewing opportunities just minutes from Reno and Las Vegas and throughout the state's unspoiled backcountry.

More than 140 natural areas were considered for the Nevada Wildlife Viewing Guide, and stringent standards were used to evaluate and choose fifty-five of them. Almost every Nevada county is represented. Many worthy sites were not included due to space, and one was eliminated in order to protect wildlife and habitat from damage. Several of the sites, such as national wildlife refuges, were acquired to protect prime wildlife habitat or vulnerable species. These sites allow viewing without causing harm to either the land or wildlife.

The sites in this viewing guide help celebrate Nevada's biological diversity—a reference to the state's rich variety of animals, plants, habitats, and ecosystems. Several full-page illustrations highlight common land features. The accompanying text explains their role in the water cycle and describes how wildlife species interact with plants, soil, and other elements of each environment.

Whether your destination is a half-acre pool with endangered springfish or a 570,000-acre high desert refuge, you will have many opportunities for memorable wildlife viewing experiences and to see the conservation of Nevada's wildlife resources in action. May these also inspire you to support agencies and private organizations working to safeguard Nevada's wildlife and wildlands legacy.

THE NATIONAL WATCHABLE WILDLIFE PROGRAM

Outstanding wildlife viewing opportunities exist in Nevada because so much of the state is publically owned land. For many years, state wildlife programs and some federal programs have been funded largely by sportsmen through license fees and federal excise taxes. These sportsmen-funded wildlife management areas, preserves, refuges, preservation programs, and habitat enhancement activities clearly benefit scores of nongame species, as well.

Today, hunting and fishing-related revenues are declining nationwide and often cannot keep pace with the increasing costs of wildlife management programs or the threats to wildlife. Conversely, wildlife viewing activities on public lands have increased significantly. Historically, however, people involved with hiking, birding, photography, and other wildlife-viewing activities have not funded site operations or wildlife programs.

The Nevada Watchable Wildlife Project is part of a national response to the increasing interest in wildlife viewing and the need to develop new support for wildlife programs. As part of the National Watchable Wildlife Program, coordinated by the Defenders of Wildlife, seven government agencies and private organizations in Nevada joined forces and funds to promote wildlife viewing, conservation, and education. The Nevada Wildlife Viewing Guide is an important step in this effort.

This book is much more than a guide; the sites are part of a wildlife viewing network. Travel routes to each site will be marked with the brown and white binocular sign shown on the cover of this book. Travelers may also notice these signs in other states. Eventually, the United States will be linked by a network of wildlife viewing sites, as similar partnerships are formed in other states.

The partnership that formed to produce the Nevada guide and viewing network will continue to work on site development, interpretation, and conservation education. Several new wildlife-viewing and conservation programs are evolving, including the USDA Forest Service's Eyes on Wildlife and the Watchable Wildlife programs offered by the Nevada Department of Wildlife, Bureau of Land Management, and US Fish and Wildlife Service.

Use this guide to plan outings that coincide with peak wildlife viewing periods. Consult it, while traveling, for interesting side trips. Take advantage of on-site education programs. And finally, support wildlife agency and private efforts to fund and conserve wildlife programs by becoming an active partner in resource stewardship.

THE GREAT BASIN DESERT

The vast Great Basin Desert covers parts of five states, including two-thirds of Nevada. John C. Frémont observed the region's basic character during his travels and named this sprawling expanse the Great Basin because its streams and lakes drain inward; none is connected to the ocean or to any of the nation's great rivers.

The region's contours have been shaped by glaciers, volcanoes, earthquakes, rainstorms, and spring runoff. It is an arid, corrugated land of more than one hundred basins separated by nearly 150 mountain ranges. It lies in the rainshadow of the Sierra Nevada and Cascade ranges. These ranges shield the Great Basin from Pacific storms and leave Nevada with cold winters, hot summers, and less rainfall than any other state.

Great Basin plant communities and the wildlife they support are very much the product of water cycles set in motion by the rainshadow effect. Clouds pass over the Sierra crest and absorb moisture from the Great Basin. When the clouds meet Nevada mountain ranges, they drop rain and snow in the high subalpine regions.

In spring, runoff filters down sagebrush-covered sideslopes and fills canyon streams defined by a corridor of lush vegetation. Water from spring runoff or summer rainstorms eventually flows into the flat-floored playa below, transforming this dry lake bed into a vast, shallow, short-lived lake. Summer heat and high winds draw moisture from the playa, leaving behind an arid landscape and perpetuating a water cycle that has tempered and shaped the land.

11

VIEWING ETHICS

Honor the rights of private landowners. Gain permission from private landowners before entering their property.

Honor the rights of others who are enjoying the viewing experience. Loud noises, quick movements, or other inappropriate behavior might frighten wildlife. Please wait your turn with patience and consideration.

Honor natural communities and processes. Please do not touch, feed, or move too close to wildlife, or their nests or dens. Leave seemingly abandoned wildlife alone. If you believe an animal is injured, sick, or abandoned, contact the nearest wildlife agency.

Honor your own right and the rights of others to enjoy the outdoors in the future. Leave Nevada's wildlands in better condition than you found them. Pick up any litter you encounter, and dispose of it properly.

VIEWING HINTS

Some of the sites in this guide offer easy wildlife viewing, while other will require both patience and knowledge of wildlife behavior. Some sites have visitor centers, interpretive trails, and educational programs; many others have no trails, no interpretation, and no facilities. Please consider these factors when selecting areas to visit. Here are some viewing tips that may increase your viewing success:

Choose your season. Some of Nevada's wildlife can be seen only at certain times of year. Some may congregate during specific seasons, their numbers making viewing much easier. Large herds of mule deer and Rocky Mountain elk are highly visible in fall and winter. White pelicans at Anaho Island are present from March to October only. Some animals hibernate through winter; others may remain hidden during hot summer days.

Watch in the early morning and near dusk. There is generally more wildlife activity in the first and last hours of daylight than any other time of day. Morning and late afternoon sunlight also provides rich, warm colors that make beautiful photographs. Remember, some species are nocturnal.

Move slowly and quietly. Increase your odds of seeing wildlife by slowing down, and stopping frequently. Allow for periods of silence before moving again. Animals often disappear as you arrive, but may return shortly if you are quiet. Use your ears to locate birds, or other vocal wildlife.

Use binoculars. A good pair of binoculars or a spotting scope will open up a whole new world of wildlife viewing. With a twenty-power spotting scope, for example, it's possible to watch a desert bighorn sheep standing 1.5 miles away.

Use field guides. Field guides include information on the habitats each animal prefers, its coloration and markings, and what it eats. Guides are available for virtually every type of plant, fish, or animal found in Nevada.

Increase viewing success by concealing yourself. Stand behind a bush, tree, or vehicle. Wear clothing colors that blend in with the environment.

Remember, some wildlife species are dangerous. Nevada is home to rattlesnakes, mountain lions, and black bears. Be aware that these animals can be nearby, and maintain a safe distance if you encounter them.

Be patient. Allow enough time for your visit. If you expect to see the featured species during a brief visit, you will likely be disappointed.

Come prepared. Many wildlife viewing sites in Nevada are very remote and have no facilities. ALWAYS CARRY WATER, FOOD, EXTRA CLOTHING, AND A GOOD MAP. DRESS APPROPRIATELY. BE SURE TO CHECK YOUR FUEL SUPPLY, AND NOTE THE CLOSEST TOWN WITH GAS OR DIESEL.

HOW TO USE THIS GUIDE

This guide is divided into five sections that correspond to the Department of Tourism's travel regions. Color strips on the edges of the pages help identify and differentiate the five regions. Wildlife viewing sites are listed and located on a highway map that introduces each region. The sites are numbered consecutively from one to fifty-five, beginning in the northwestern part of the state.

Each site contains the following elements to help describe and interpret what may be seen:

Wildlife Icons: These symbols show the types of animals and plants that are likely to be seen or are unique to the site. They do not include all species at the site.

Description: A brief account of the featured wildlife and habitats. This provides viewers with hints of where to look and what to look for.

Viewing Information: Describes the site's featured wildlife, the reliability of viewing, and best viewing seasons. This section may include interesting facts or viewing tips. IMPORTANT NOTES CONCERNING SITE RESTRICTIONS, SAFETY, AND VIEWING CONDITIONS ARE NOTED IN CAPITAL LETTERS.

Directions: In most cases, both written directions and a site map are provided. Occasionally, when two sites appear on facing pages, one map will be used to show both sites. Do not rely entirely on these maps. Many sites in Nevada are remote or located off unmarked dirt roads; it is essential to carry good regional, county, BLM, or USFS maps.

Site Manager: Provides the abbreviated name of the agency or organization that manages the site. Several driving tours involve viewing on private lands from public roads and pullouts. Please respect private property signs and other warnings.

Telephone Number: Appears after the site manager, to provide more information about the site.

Size: Refers to the size in acres or in miles if it is a driving tour.

Closest Town: Suggests the closest town for reliable fuel. These towns may not always carry diesel fuel.

Recreation and Facilities Symbols: Provide information about some of the facilities and opportunities available at each site. Please note that the barrier-free symbol means that there is at least car viewing and one barrier-free rest room on site. Please call for more detailed information.

SITE OWNER/MANAGER ABBREVIATIONS

BLM—US Bureau of Land Management
BOR—US Bureau of Reclamation
NDOW—Nevada Department of Wildlife
NDSP—Nevada Division of State Parks
NPS—National Park Service
PVT—Privately owned land
USFWS—US Fish & Wildlife Service
USFS—USDA Forest Service

FEATURED WILDLIFE

Songbirds, Perching Birds | Upland Birds | Shorebirds | Raptors Birds of Prey | Aquatic Birds | Wading Birds

Waterfowl | Freshwater Mammals | Fish | Reptiles, Amphibians | Bats | Wildflowers

Hoofed Mammals | Carnivores | Small Mammals | Insects

FACILITIES AND RECREATION

Parking | Restrooms Pit Toilets | Barrier-free | Picinic | Drinking Water | Hiking

Entry Fee | Camping | Bicycling | Cross-country Skiing | Horse Trails | Non-Motorized Boats

Lodging | Restaurants | Boat Ramp | Motorized Boats

HIGHWAY SIGNS

As you travel in Nevada and other states, look for these binocular signs on interstates, highways, and other roads. They identify the route to wildlife viewing sites.

FALCON PRESS

BUSINESS REPLY MAIL

FIRST-CLASS MAIL PERMIT NO 80 HELENA MT

POSTAGE WILL BE PAID BY ADDRESSEE

FALCON PRESS PUBLISHING CO
PO BOX 1718
HELENA MT 59624-9948

NEVADA MAP

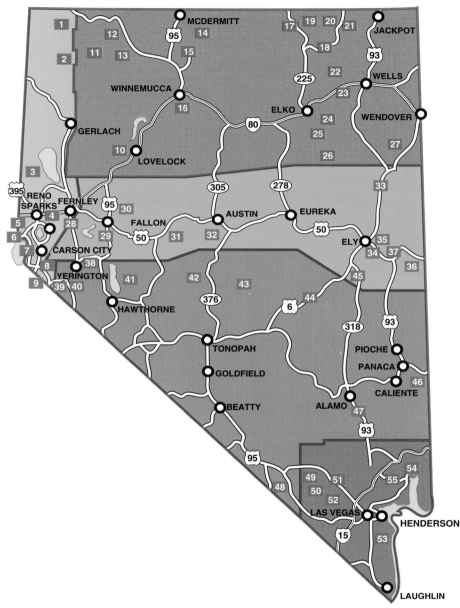

MAP INFORMATION

Nevada's wildlife viewing sites have been organized into five regions, using names adopted by the Nevada Department of Tourism. Each region is introduced by a full-page map showing major roads and cities, as well as the location of each wildlife viewing site.

REGION ONE: RENO TAHOE TERRITORY

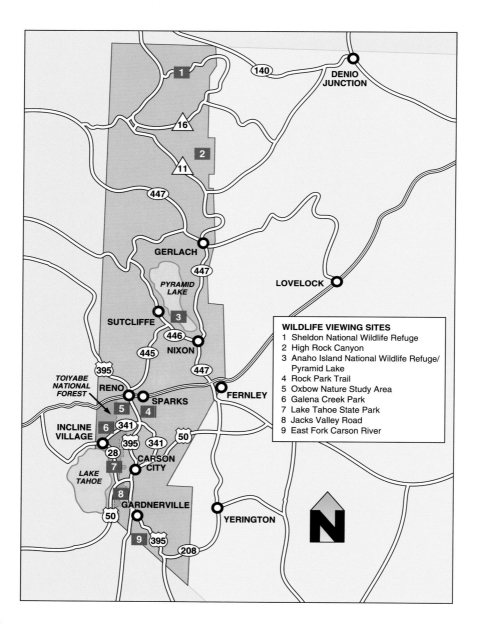

WILDLIFE VIEWING SITES
1 Sheldon National Wildlife Refuge
2 High Rock Canyon
3 Anaho Island National Wildlife Refuge/
   Pyramid Lake
4 Rock Park Trail
5 Oxbow Nature Study Area
6 Galena Creek Park
7 Lake Tahoe State Park
8 Jacks Valley Road
9 East Fork Carson River

Description: Vast expanses of big and low sagebrush are broken by outcrops of rimrock and steep gorges—rugged country where golden eagles, prairie falcons, and American kestrels hunt. Scattered springs, lakes, and creeks draw eighty percent of refuge wildlife, including frogs and toads. Canada geese, mallards, gadwalls, and other ducks share Dufurrena Ponds, Catnip Reservoir, and Big Spring with killdeer and Wilson's phalaropes. Sage grouse, California quail, and chukars are common; look for grouse and their chicks in wet meadows during spring and summer. Hundreds of pronghorn winter at Big Springs and Gooch Tables, then pass spring and summer at Swan Lake. Mule deer winter on the eastern refuge, and by summer have moved up to higher elevations. Hikers may spot bighorn sheep on the remote ridges of Hell Creek and McGee Mountain. Reptiles inhabit the rocky terrain at Virgin Valley, Jackass Flat, and Bog Hot, named for its hot springs. Coyotes, jackrabbits, and ground squirrels are common.

Viewing Information: Watch near water, also along CR 16 and CR 11. More than 175 bird species. Waterfowl viewing excellent in spring and fall, when water present. Songbirds and birds of prey are plentiful, spring through fall. Excellent viewing of upland game, small mammals, pronghorn, mule deer, and bighorn sheep spring through fall. REMOTE AREA. CARRY FOOD, WATER, FUEL. HIGH CLEARANCE VEHICLE RECOMMENDED. ROADS SOMETIMES IMPASSABLE FALL THROUGH SPRING. CALL FOR ROAD CONDITIONS.

Directions: From Denio Junction, take SR 140 west twenty-five miles to refuge entrance sign and turn left (south) on gravel road. Drive one mile to Dufurrena Field Station. Get information here or at Virgin Valley Campground, one mile beyond field station. SEE MAP.

Site Manager: USFWS (503) 947-3315
Size: 571,000 acres
Closest Town: Denio Junction, twenty-five miles

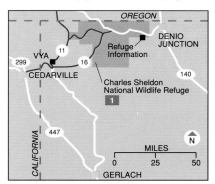

2 | HIGH ROCK CANYON

Description: AUTO TOUR. This trip begins near High Rock Lake, then winds through a rugged canyon. High Rock Lake attracts many spring migrants, including tundra swans and killdeer. Steep canyon walls shelter nests used by golden eagles, great horned owls, red-tailed hawks, American kestrels, and prairie falcons. Cliff crevices and holes provide habitat for roosting bats and nesting white-throated swifts. Brushy areas and riparian thickets offer views of calliope hummingbirds, lazuli buntings, and green-tailed towhees. Wrens, sparrows, snakes, and lizards are common. Watch among the mountain mahogany and sagebrush for sage grouse, mule deer, coyotes, and pronghorn.

Viewing Information: Many pull-outs. Excellent year-round views of birds of prey, coyotes, and small mammals. Songbird, bat, reptile viewing excellent spring through fall. Deer and pronghorn are best seen spring and summer. Camping, viewing at Steven's Camp. REMOTE SITE. 4WD VEHICLE REQUIRED. TAKE FOOD, WATER, FUEL. ROADS OFTEN IMPASSABLE IN WINTER AND EARLY SPRING. CANYON CLOSED FEBRUARY 1 TO APRIL 15.

Directions: *From Gerlach, drive north on CR 11, a gravel road. After driving forty-four miles, turn right on Smokey Canyon Road, and drive fifteen miles. Turn northwest at High Rock Lake and begin tour. Drive seventeen miles through canyon to Steven's Camp, then continue twelve miles to CR 16.* SEE MAP.

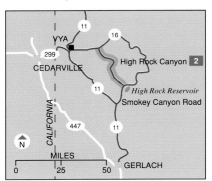

Site Manager: BLM (916) 279-6101
Size: Twenty-nine-mile drive
Closest Town: Cedarville, CA, thirty-seven miles

The fast-moving prairie falcon is most often seen flying close to the ground, watching for rodents and ground-nesting birds. Pesticide residues in some prey species may cause thin egg shells and poor hatching success among the falcons.
GEORGE WUERTHNER

3 | ANAHO ISLAND NATIONAL WILDLIFE REFUGE - PYRAMID LAKE

Description: Located off the east shore of Pyramid Lake, Anaho Island hosts one of the largest white pelican nesting colonies in North America. Sand and gravel benches dotted with greasewood provide nesting sites for double-crested cormorants, Caspian terns, California gulls, and great blue herons. Western grebes, common loons, and ospreys often fish in the offshore waters. Tundra swans and waterfowl are common in fall and winter. Shorelines and uplands offer views of black-tailed jackrabbits, Great Basin kangaroo rats, and occasional coyotes.

Viewing Information: ISLAND CLOSED TO PUBLIC. View from a boat or east shoreline; use binoculars or a spotting scope for best results. Pelicans visible March to October; they often feed near south shore. Waterfowl viewing is excellent year-round; grebes, loons, gulls, shorebirds, and wading birds present spring through fall. Golden eagles and other hawks are common year-round. Lizards and wildflowers best in spring and summer. More viewing on west shore, from south lake to Sutcliff Marina. Facilities at marina and Pelican Point. Lake and shoreline owned by Paiute Tribe. Fee camping. AVOID SOFT SAND ADJACENT TO ROADS. BOATING DANGEROUS IN HIGH WINDS.

Directions: *From Nixon, take SR 447 north 7.5 miles and turn west on dirt road. Travel seven miles to east side viewing area.* SEE MAP.

Site Manager: Paiute Tribe (702) 476-1155; USFWS (702) 423-5128
Size: 700 acres
Closest Town: Fernley, thirty-three miles

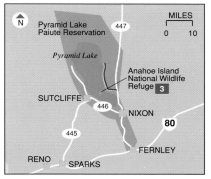

During spring, Anaho Island shelters one of North America's largest white pelican nesting populations. These colonial nesters and their young find safety in large numbers. The island setting also helps eliminate some predators and other disturbances.
JIM STAMATES

19

4 ROCK PARK TRAIL

Description: URBAN SITE. A ten-foot wide, paved trail meanders through the riparian corridor along the Truckee River. Throughout the year mallards, wood ducks, mergansers, and other waterfowl feed and preen in the water. Great blue herons wade along the shore, watching for trout, suckers, and other fish. Beavers use well-worn earthen slides along the banks to join muskrats in the river; both build riverbank dens. Streamside cottonwoods shelter Mexican freetail bats and the nests of northern orioles and scrub jays. Many birds of prey perch high in the leafy canopy, watching for rabbits, squirrels, and other small mammals. Low shrubs hide the nests of goldfinches and other songbirds. Bullfrogs call from the shallows, while gopher snakes and lizards hide under rocks and fallen trees.

Viewing Information: Excellent barrier-free access. Enjoy excellent year-round views of small mammals and waterfowl. Outstanding views of birds of prey, songbirds, wading birds, and aquatic mammals spring through fall. Kill-deer visit in spring and summer. Good viewing of reptiles and amphibians spring through fall.

Directions: In Sparks, from Interstate 80, turn south on Rock Blvd. (Exit 17) and continue to Rock Park. SEE MAP.

Site Manager: City of Sparks (702) 353-2376
Size: Three-mile trail
Closest Town: Sparks

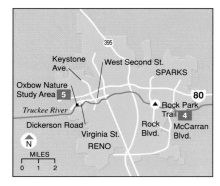

From their uppermost branches inhabited by birds of prey and songbirds, to their massive roots mined by the burrows of squirrels and other mammals, streamside cottonwoods along the Rock Park Trail are a focal point for wildlife.
KENNETH L. MILLER

5 ■ OXBOW NATURE STUDY AREA

Description: URBAN SITE. The sandbars, small islands, and ponds along an oxbow bend of the Truckee River support a diversity of wildlife at this site, located in the heart of Reno. Herring gulls and ospreys glide over three secluded riverside viewing decks. Approach quietly to catch a glimpse of Canada geese, great blue herons, wood ducks, mergansers, even minks. Muskrats are usually visible along the river and by Doyle Island, where beavers dams have formed a shallow wetland. Listen here for bullfrogs and watch for tiger swallowtail butterflies. Monarch butterflies feed among the milkweed. Tall cottonwoods shelter tree swallows, northern orioles, evening and black-headed grosbeaks, broad-tailed hummingbirds, and many finches. Red-winged and yellow-headed blackbirds reside among cattails lining an inland pond.

Viewing Information: More than 100 bird species. Interpretive Center open by appointment. Outstanding year-round views of muskrats, and songbirds such as cedar waxwings and Anna's hummingbirds. Excellent viewing of waterfowl, amphibians, and birds of prey spring through fall; osprey appear in spring and fall. Spring and summer are best for wading birds, turtles, butterflies, and wildflowers. Excellent barrier-free access.

Directions: In Reno, from Interstate 80, take Keystone Avenue (Exit 12) south. Turn west on West Second Street and drive .75 miles. Turn southwest onto Dickerson Road and continue to entrance. SEE MAP OPPOSITE PAGE.

Site Manager: NDOW, City of Reno (702) 688-1893
Size: Eight acres
Closest Town: located in Reno

The yellow-headed blackbird is a gregarious marsh songster known for large nesting colonies. Look among tall pond vegetation for its tightly-woven spring nests.
JAN L. WASSINK

21

6 GALENA CREEK PARK

Description: Water sweeps down heavily forested Mount Rose and funnels into Galena Creek, leaving behind fan-shaped deposits of rocks and boulders. Snakes and lizards hide among the rock crevices. Aspens, alders, and dogwoods border the creek and shelter raccoons, rufous-sided towhees, and migratory mountain chickadees, yellow-warblers, and other songbirds. On warm days, a vanilla scent emanates from Jeffrey pines inhabited by resident Steller's jays, with Clark's nutcrackers in fall. Ponderosa pines serve as lookouts for red-tailed hawks and other birds of prey. Watch for hairy woodpeckers, northern flickers, and red-breasted sapsuckers. The understory shelters mule deer, golden-mantled ground squirrels, raccoons, and coyotes. Black bears feed on the abundant bittercherry. Bears, bobcats, owls, and bats are nocturnal residents here. A one-mile nature trail explores the park.

Viewing Information: Good year-round views of jays, woodpeckers, small mammals. Birds of prey and songbirds are best seen spring and fall. Good viewing of warblers, leopard frogs, tree frogs, water snakes, and reptiles along creek. Many trails. Fair barrier-free access. Tours for ten or more by appointment only. CALL AHEAD FOR ROAD OR PARK CLOSURES.

Directions: From Reno, drive south on US Highway 395 six miles to SR 431 (Mt. Rose Highway). Turn west and drive seven miles to park entrances. SEE MAP.

Site Manager: Washoe County Parks (702) 849-2511
Size: 420 acres
Closest Town: Reno, thirteen miles

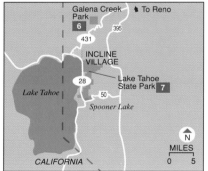

Identified by its deep blue body, prominent dark crest, and harsh calls, the Steller's jay is a common and conspicuous resident of the conifer forest.
LEONARD LEE RUE III

7 LAKE TAHOE STATE PARK

Description: This rugged, forested park spans elevations of 6,200 to 8,900 feet and includes three miles of shoreline with stunning lake vistas. The highway and parking areas offer lake views of common mergansers, mallards, ospreys, and bald eagles. Watch wildlife from Spooner Lake's 1.5-mile nature trail, or take a rigorous sixteen-mile trail, which begins at Spooner Lake, skirts Marlette Reservoir, and ends at Hidden Beach. Throughout the park watch for mule deer, chickadees, and chipmunks. Scan the conifers for Cooper's hawks, northern goshawks, warblers, thrushes, and nuthatches. Occasional old-growth stands shelter Williamson's sapsuckers, white-headed woodpeckers, and other cavity nesters. Blue grouse hide in the understory. Watch for band-tailed pigeons in flight. Coyote sightings are common, but the Sierra Nevada red fox remains elusive.

Viewing Information: Good to excellent viewing of all wildlife spring through fall. Excellent spring and summer wildflowers, butterflies. See Lahontan cut-throat as broodstock and spawning in summer at Marlette Reservoir. Heavy winter snow. Located on Tahoe Rim Trail. SOME TRAILS CHALLENGING. BEWARE OF SLIDES, DEBRIS, HIKERS, BIKERS, AND HORSES.

Directions: *From Carson City on Highway 50, drive west thirteen miles to SR 28 and turn right (north). Drive .7 miles on SR 28 to Spooner Lake entrance.* SEE MAP OPPOSITE PAGE.

Site Manager: NDSP (702) 831-0494
Size: 13,500 acres
Closest Town: Incline Village, eight miles

Many Lake Tahoe-area wildlife species are seasonally abundant but very secretive. Observe them with binoculars from high-elevation trails, near secluded beaches, or along the rocky shoreline.
GEORGE WEURTHNER

23

8 JACKS VALLEY ROAD

Description: AUTO TOUR. Drive or bicycle twenty-two miles through prime deer winter range in this picturesque valley. Hundreds of mule deer pass through here to feed on bitterbrush, sagebrush, and agricultural fields. Keen observers may be able to differentiate between the subspecies: Nevada's Rocky Mountain mule deer have a black tip on their white tails, while California mule deer have more black on their tails—often a black line running the length of the tail. During the drive, watch fence posts and utility poles for red-tailed hawks, northern harriers, and occasional bald eagles and Swainson's hawks. Canada geese may be spotted feeding in fields or at ranch ponds.

Viewing Information: Deer present mid-October through April; excellent viewing in winter. Deer are best seen early mornings or after 4 p.m.; please remain in vehicle or on bike to minimize disturbance. Birds of prey use valley all year but numbers peak in winter. Canada geese are present fall through spring. Many historical markers. Facilities at Mormon Station Historic Monument.

Directions: *From Carson City, take US Highway 395 south three miles. Turn west on SR 206 and drive twenty-two miles, meeting SR 88 ten miles south of Minden.* SEE MAP.

Site Manager: PVT (702) 688-1500
Size: Twenty-two-mile drive
Closest Town: Carson City, three miles

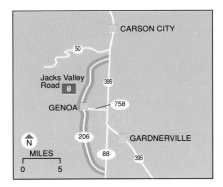

During fall and early winter, mule deer bucks fight to determine which males will breed. Heavy snows eventually drive high-country deer herds to lower elevation winter range, such as Jack's Valley, where forage is still abundant.
CHASE SWIFT

Description: RIVER VIEWING. Take a twenty-one-mile raft or kayak trip through an unspoiled river canyon lined by sagebrush, pinyon pines, and steep, craggy cliffs. Rock holes and ledges are used by cliff-nesting swallows. American dippers and belted kingfishers feed in the river. Canada geese, mergansers, and great blue herons are common. Look for heron nests among the cottonwoods, and red-tailed hawks and turkey vultures perched in the upper branches. Watch for northern flickers feeding on the ground, and hairy and downy woodpeckers in the pinyon pines and cottonwoods. Coyotes and mule deer move between open areas and the river, where riparian vegetation shelters nuthatches and other songbirds. Watch near shore for mink and other small mammals.

Viewing Information: Viewing best in May; good during spring and early summer. Watch for mammals early morning and late afternoon. Trip takes seven hours. Commercial raft trips available. CALL AHEAD; DAILY WATER FLOWS FLUCTUATE. WATER VERY COLD. BE SURE TO TAKE OUT UP-STREAM OF RUHENSTROTH DAM'S FORTY- TO SIXTY-FOOT FALLS.

Directions: Put-in at Hangman's Bridge, one mile east of Markleeville, CA. Take-out is upstream from pump station above Washoe Tribe Campground, six miles south of Gardnerville. SEE MAP.

Site Manager: USFS (702) 882-2766
Size: Twenty-one-mile float trip
Closest Town: Markleeville, CA, one mile

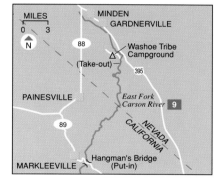

Known for its tendency to take a "dip" in order to forage, the American dipper is closely associated with rivers and streams. Special scales cover its eyes while it dives, swims, and runs under swift-moving water. Look under overhanging stream banks for its nest.
C. ALLAN MORGAN

25

REGION TWO: COWBOY COUNTRY

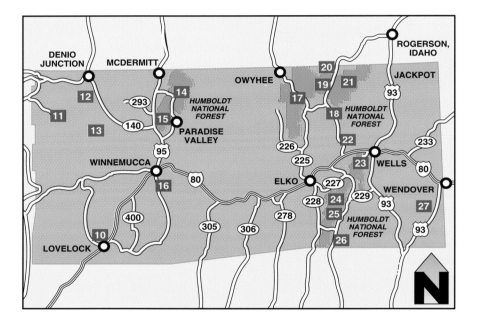

WILDLIFE VIEWING SITES
10 Lovelock Valley
11 Mahogany Creek
12 Pine Forest Mountains
13 McGill Canyon
14 Santa Rosa Mountains
15 Summit Trail
16 Sonoma Creek
17 Wildhorse Crossing Campground
18 Bruneau Meadows
19 Bear Creek Summit
20 Jarbidge Canyon
21 Biroth Ridge
22 Cabin Field
23 Angel Lake
24 Lamoille Canyon National Scenic Byway
25 Ruby Crest National Recreational Trail
26 Ruby Lake National Wildlife Refuge
27 Goshute Mountains

Description: AUTO TOUR. Paved country roads border farms and ranches whose fertile fields and cottonwood boundaries support a wealth of wildlife. Deer mice and other small mammals inhabit fields and draw high numbers of wintering birds of prey, including northern harriers, rough-legged hawks, ferruginous hawks, golden eagles, prairie falcons, great horned owls, short-eared owls, and red-tailed hawks—look for these birds soaring or perched on utility poles and in tall trees. Open fields may also provide views of mule deer, ring-necked pheasants, California quail, and coyotes. Willows and Russian olives shelter a variety of orioles, warblers, thrushes, and porcupines. Several species of lizards and snakes may be spotted, including the rare red coachwhip snake.

Viewing Information: Excellent car or bicycle viewing on tour route and from other Lovelock public roads. Birds of prey are featured; outstanding winter viewing. Songbirds, small mammals, reptiles, and many butterflies are visible spring through fall. Good views of upland birds and porcupines all year. PLEASE RESPECT PRIVATE PROPERTY AND OWNERS' PRIVACY. USE PULL-OUTS WHEN STOPPING.

Directions: *At Lovelock and Interstate 80, take Exit 107 south into Lovelock. Turn left on 14th Street, then turn left on Lovelock Valley Road. Continue for 1.3 miles, then veer northwest onto Loorz Road. Begin viewing. Continue one mile to Fairview Road and turn left. Drive one mile, then turn left on N. Meridian Road. Continue two miles into Lovelock.* SEE MAP.

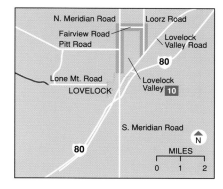

Site Manager: PVT (702) 423-3171
Size: Four-mile drive
Closest Town: Lovelock, one mile

Bird of prey migration is triggered by fall's first cold front and continues with each new wave of cold weather. This short-eared owl joins hundreds of other wintering raptors near Lovelock.
SCOTT PRICE

27

11 MAHOGANY CREEK

Description: Bounded by wet meadows and corridors of aspens and willows, this high mountain creek in big sagebrush country supports spawning populations of Lahontan cutthroat trout. No fishing is allowed, but spawning can be observed in April and May. Primitive hiking trails penetrate riparian growth inhabited by many resident and migratory songbirds, including mountain bluebirds, yellow warblers, hermit thrushes, and red-naped sapsuckers. Look in seeps or along banks for Pacific treefrogs and Great Basin spadefoot toads. Chukars, sage grouse, and ground squirrels leave their sagebrush cover to feed in open spaces and meadows, where northern goshawks, Cooper's hawks, and red-tailed hawks patrol overhead. Coyotes are active during the day; the evening hunt is left to long-eared owls, bobcats, and mountain lions. Look for mule deer near the creek or along the margins of mountain mahogany stands. Pronghorn favor sagebrush-covered benches.

Viewing Information: Unspoiled site with excellent chance to see fish spawning in spring. Very reliable viewing of most other species spring through fall. Amphibians, butterflies, wildflowers best viewed spring and summer. No winter viewing. VERY REMOTE. 4WD RECOMMENDED. BRING MAP, WATER, FOOD, FUEL, OTHER EMERGENCY EQUIPMENT. BEWARE OF RATTLESNAKES.

Directions: SEE MAP.
Site Manager: BLM (702) 623-1500
Size: 12,300 acres
Closest Town: Denio Junction, forty miles

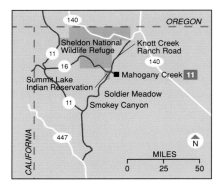

Mahogany Creek is one of northern Nevada's best examples of a high quality riparian system and prime Lahontan cutthroat trout habitat. The threatened trout spawn among gravels in the clear creek water.
KENNETH L. MILLER

12 | PINE FOREST MOUNTAINS

Description and Directions: AUTO TOUR. This drive begins fourteen miles south of Denio Junction, at SR 140 and the Blue Lake turnoff. It climbs toward rugged granite spires flanked by high-elevation meadows and lakes. Sage thrashers, California quail, and jackrabbits inhabit foothill sagebrush. Roadside utility poles are often occupied by golden eagles and American kestrels. Pass through the Alta Creek drainage, watching open areas for chukars; scan northern slopes for California bighorn sheep and mule deer. Pronghorn frequent flatlands between the maintenance station and canyon mouth. A large meadow beyond some stone homesteads attracts mule deer and sage grouse. Look aloft for northern harriers, red-tailed hawks, and other birds of prey. The road climbs the spine of Pine Forest Mountain, offering spectacular views. Meadowlarks, mountain bluebirds, and other songbirds inhabit the aspen-lined basins. Hikers should detour to Blue Lake and take a one-mile hike to clear, sapphire lakes—mule deer, yellow-bellied marmots, and coyotes may be spotted here. The tour continues to Onion Valley Reservoir, populated by occasional waterfowl and shorebirds. East slope aspens here turn vibrant yellow and orange in fall. Continue through the Alder Creek drainage, watching for mule deer and pronghorn, then descend to Gridley Lake. This slender, spring-fed playa is a late spring staging area for many waterfowl and shorebirds, particularly snowy plovers. Burrowing owls inhabit the low desert flats. From here, continue north and reconnect with SR 140. SEE MAP BELOW.

Viewing Information: Summer and fall are the only viewing seasons, with good chances of seeing all featured species. June and early July visitors will see many wildflowers. Water birds present only when lakes have water. Primitive facilities at Onion Valley. REMOTE AREA; BRING FUEL, FOOD, WATER. DIRT ROADS; 4WD ADVISED. ROADS PASSABLE ONLY IN DRY WEATHER.

Site Manager: BLM (702) 623-1500
Size: Twenty-four-mile drive
Closest Town: Denio Junction, fourteen miles

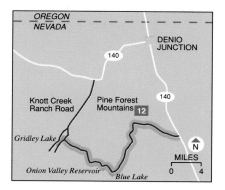

Loggerhead shrike

Great Basin Landscapes: The Playa

Over time, streams and runoff deposit rocks, soil, and debris along the base of many mountain ranges. These deposits, called alluvial fans, extend into one of the most common Great Basin features: the playa, or dry lake bed.

The playa's cracked clay or salt-encrusted flats may seem barren, but they are only dormant. Spores, seeds, and eggs lie in the dried mud, and spring runoff or summer rains will bring them to life. When water is present, the playa becomes a bountiful place that attracts migratory shorebirds, waterfowl, and other wildlife.

Most of the year, however, the playa is dry. Plants and animals must cope with minimal moisture, sizzling daytime temperatures, salty soils, and drying winds. Some plants have special mechanisms for secreting excessive salts, while others have tap roots dozens of feet in length. Many desert plants have small, narrow leaves, or shed their leaves to limit moisture loss. Waxy surfaces or dull colors also help reduce evaporation. Some plants are succulent, with the ability to absorb and store water.

Surviving the desert's harsh conditions is easier for animals, which simply move to avoid heat or find sustenance. Birds follow shade created by plants. Mammals avoid daytime heat in underground dens. The desert tortoise will sleep for months at a time in a cool, underground burrow.

Most birds and mammals feed in the mornings, evenings, or entirely at night to avoid the heat. They receive moisture from the food they eat, or by visiting a nearby waterhole. The kangaroo rat lives entirely on the moisture found in seeds. Bighorn sheep can survive without water for several days. The antelope ground squirrel can forage longer on hot days by bending its tail forward, like an umbrella, to create its own portable source of shade.

13 McGILL CANYON

Description: Jagged limestone ridges and outcroppings tower above this narrow canyon, sheltering California bighorn sheep and mule deer. Golden eagles, prairie falcons, and red-tailed hawks ride air currents, scanning the sagebrush and juniper basin below for black-tailed jackrabbits, cottontails, and ground squirrels. Sage grouse, chukars, and mourning doves also inhabit the grassy basin. Streamside vegetation provides cover for warblers, wrens, hummingbirds, along with occasional porcupines and long-tailed weasels. Watch for yellow-bellied marmots in rocky areas, and rock wrens in crevice nests above. Coyotes and kit foxes may be spotted hunting by day; mountain lions and bobcats are active night hunters.

Viewing Information: Excellent viewing of bighorn sheep, deer, and upland birds year-round. Bighorn lambing March-April on high slopes; please do not disturb. Good viewing of predators, birds of prey, and reptiles year-round. Small mammals and songbirds are present spring through fall. Many spring wildflowers. VERY REMOTE, RUGGED SITE WITH NO FACILITIES. TAKE FOOD, WATER, FUEL. NO MAINTAINED ROADS OR HIKING TRAILS. RATTLESNAKES PRESENT SPRING THROUGH FALL.

Directions: From Winnemucca, take US Highway 95 north thirty-one miles and turn west on SR 140. Drive thirty-five miles northwest to Leonard Creek Road and turn west. Drive 7.5 miles to end of pavement. Continue south nineteen miles to canyon. SEE MAP.

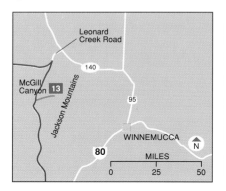

Site Manager: BLM (702) 623-1500
Size: 3,500 acres
Closest Town: Denio Junction, thirty-nine miles

The massive, curved horns of this muscular bighorn ram bear annular rings, like a tree, that correspond to his age. The California bighorn sheep found at McGill Canyon are one of three subspecies that reside in Nevada.
DAVID K. ROSEN

14 SANTA ROSA MOUNTAINS

Description and Directions: AUTO TOUR. Bighorn sheep, mule deer, and ruffed grouse inhabit this desert mountain tour. From Winnemucca, take US Highway 95 north twenty-two miles. Turn right on SR 290 and continue eighteen miles to Paradise Valley. Follow SR 792 along Indian Creek (road later called FR 084). Switchback up Hinkey Summit; watch for mule deer, chukars, yellow-bellied marmots, and spring wildflowers. Golden eagles often soar near spectacular rock outcroppings to the east. Look for northern goshawks above aspen pockets inhabited by ruffed grouse, red-shafted flickers, and many songbirds. Pass streams with Lahontan cutthroat trout and wet meadows visited by deer and great blue herons. Look for pronghorn and sage grouse on the plateaus. At Windy Gap, scan rocky outcrops for California bighorn sheep, then drop down through the site of a recent wildfire, where new grasses attract deer, bighorn sheep, and chukars. Descend through Quinn Valley and connect with US Highway 95 sixteen miles north of Orovada. SEE MAP BELOW.

Viewing Information: Good to excellent viewing of featured species spring through fall. Watch for bighorns and deer in early morning or late afternoon. Ruffed grouse drum noisily in spring. Nesting and fledgling birds present April to September. Fee camping. SINGLE LANE GRAVEL ROAD. ROUGH SWITCHBACKS TO SUMMITS. HIGH CLEARANCE VEHICLES RECOMMENDED. TRAILERS SHOULD BE PULLED BY 4WD.

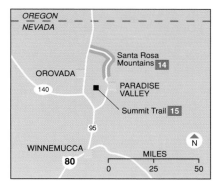

Site Manager: USFS (702) 623-5025
Size: Thirty-nine-mile drive
Closest Town: Orovada, sixteen miles

The colorful and vocal mountain bluebird is Nevada's state bird. Mountain bluebirds inhabit conifer belts and old-growth forests, often nesting in cavities abandoned by woodpeckers and other species.
CHASE SWIFT

15 SUMMIT TRAIL

Description: This twelve-mile hiking and horseback trail traverses the crest of the rugged Santa Rosa/Paradise Peak Wilderness—high country with panoramic views, abundant wildlife, and solitude. Mountain brush habitat attracts a large mule deer herd, and granite-faced peaks provide isolation for California bighorn sheep. In fall, bright pockets of aspens shelter downy woodpeckers, mountain bluebirds, and many species of warblers and wrens. Creeks teem with trout, and some stretches sustain threatened Lahontan cutthroat trout. Coyotes, yellow-bellied marmots, and sage grouse appear on low, sagebrush-covered hills. Bluebells, lupines, and other spring wildflowers border trails where the footprints of night-hunting mountain lions and bobcats can be spotted. Look skyward for northern goshawks, golden eagles, and red-tailed hawks.

Viewing Information: Good to excellent viewing of all featured species spring through fall. Deer and bighorn best seen early mornings or late afternoons. Beware of rattlesnakes. Horse unloading area one mile from road's end. FR 092 IS STEEP, NARROW, AND SLICK WHEN WET. NO FACILITIES. BRING FUEL, WATER, AND FOOD.

Directions: *From Winnemucca, take US Highway 95 north twenty-one miles. Turn right on SR 290 and drive seventeen miles to Singas Road turnoff (FR 092). Turn west and drive six miles on gravel and dirt road to trailhead. SEE MAP.*

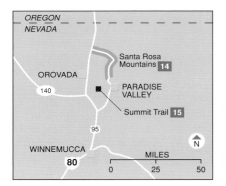

Site Manager: USFS (702) 623-5025
Size: Twelve-mile trail
Closest Town: Winnemucca, forty-four miles

The golden eagle, Nevada's most common resident bird of prey, is at home in the rolling foothills and the state's most rugged mountain terrain. Watch for these large birds soaring or perched on snags and utility poles.
LEONARD LEE RUE III

SONOMA CREEK

Description: Hide within the shelter of vegetation bordering Sonoma Creek and watch black-tailed jackrabbits, mule deer, and coyotes on the arid sideslopes. Prairie falcons, golden eagles, and American kestrels patrol the skies. The creek's leafy canopy sustains northern flickers and many songbirds, including green-tailed towhees, song sparrows, and lazuli buntings. Fallen trees and underbrush shelter chukars, long-tailed weasels, and mountain cottontails. In years of good runoff, the creek supports summer toad populations, common snipe, and waterfowl, including spring-nesting mallards. Watch near water for California quail. As part of a habitat restoration project, two portions of the stream have been fenced to protect the stream banks.

Viewing Information: Good to excellent year-round viewing of most featured species. Songbirds are abundant spring through summer. Reptiles, snakes are common spring through fall. Lots of wildlife activity within exclosure. Mule deer plentiful in early morning. Some viewing from vehicles at pull-outs. ROAD MUDDY AFTER RAIN.

Directions: In Winnemucca, from US Highway 95, turn right on Winnemucca Blvd. Drive .5 miles and turn east on Hanson Street. Turn south on Grass Valley Road. Drive eleven miles to Sonoma Creek turnoff and turn east. SEE MAP.

Site Manager: BLM (702) 623-1500
Size: 2,400 acres
Closest Town: Winnemucca, eleven miles

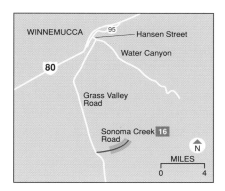

Pound for pound, the weasel is one of nature's most fearless predators. This long-tailed weasel readily challenges prey several times its own size, chasing animals up trees or down burrows.

MICHAEL S. SAMPLE

35

17 ▌WILD HORSE CROSSING CAMPGROUND

Description: A road with fifty turns parallels the Owyhee River as it winds among steep volcanic cliffs, home to nesting white-throated swifts, cliff swallows, and Say's phoebes. The campground is located on a serene stretch of the river lined by willows and aspens, and bounded by steep sagebrush slopes favored by mule deer. Fallen trees and numerous dams are evidence of beavers. Their handiwork has created wetlands occupied by mallards, common mergansers, and Canada geese. Spotted sandpipers probe the shoreline and belted kingfishers perch in riverbank willows. The aspens shelter downy woodpeckers, yellow-bellied sapsuckers, western flycatchers, mountain bluebirds, and many warblers. Look for long-tailed weasels near fallen trees and dense cover. Yellow-bellied marmots and least chipmunks may be spotted in the open. Red-tailed hawks, golden eagles, and ferruginous hawks are common. Quiet campers may spot beavers, coyotes, and great horned owls at night.

Viewing Information: Very good viewing of beaver, coyotes, small mammals, and waterfowl year-round. Deer and birds of prey are most common spring through fall. Look for songbirds and sandpipers in late spring and summer. Fee camping. Many side canyon hikes. Visit nearby Wild Horse Reservoir. WATCH FOR RATTLESNAKES NEAR RIVER BANKS.

Directions: *From Elko, drive north seventy-one miles on SR 225 to campground, which is located eight miles north of Wild Horse Reservoir Headquarters.* SEE MAP.

Site Manager: USFS (702) 763-6691
Size: Five acres
Closest Town: Mountain City, ten miles

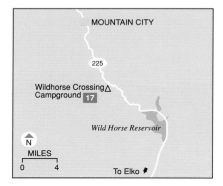

MOUNTAIN CITY

225

Wildhorse Crossing△
Campground 17

Wild Horse Reservoir

N
MILES
0   4

To Elko ✦

Seldom seen in daylight, the night-laboring beaver leaves behind gnawed trees, woven dams, and shallow ponds. From waterfowl to deer, many wildlife species rely on the riparian habitat engineered by this large rodent.
LEONARD LEE RUE III

18 BRUNEAU MEADOWS

Description: Mule deer and pronghorn often feed on the sagebrush hills or among the sedges and rushes of this wet meadow. Muskrat lodges in marshy areas serve as platforms for mallards and other ducks. During spring, look for yellow-headed blackbirds in tall marsh vegetation. Pause at pull-outs to scan the uplands for sage grouse, pygmy rabbits, coyotes, and badgers. Look aloft for prairie falcons, northern harriers, and golden eagles. Meadowlarks perch on fence posts or sagebrush; lizards and snakes bask in the open on warm days. Stop at Charleston Reservoir's south overlook to watch white pelicans, Canada geese, western grebes, and other waterfowl. Look for great blue herons, white-faced ibis, and shorebirds in the shallows.

Viewing Information: Good viewing of all featured mammals and birds of prey spring through fall; best times are early morning and late afternoon. Waterfowl, shorebirds, and songbirds excellent during spring and summer; waterfowl good in fall. Wading birds and reptiles best seen in summer. Watch for pronghorn on CR 746. No facilities. PLEASE DO NOT ENTER MEADOW OR DISTURB NESTING BIRDS. REMOTE SITE. DIRT ROADS NARROW; MAY BE IMPASSABLE DURING WINTER AND SPRING.

Directions: *From Elko, drive fifty-five miles north on SR 225. Turn east on CR 746, and drive twenty-one miles to Reservoir. Meadow is one mile south of reservoir. SEE MAP.*

Site Manager: BLM (702) 753-0200
Size: 400 acres
Closest Town: Mountain City, forty-five miles

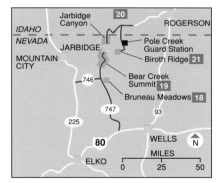

The western meadowlark is neither shy about singing nor protecting its breeding territory. A resident of grasslands, fields, and meadows, it often perches on fence posts to deliver its loud, flute-like song.
WILLIAM H. MULLINS

19 BEAR CREEK SUMMIT

Description: AUTO TOUR. From Bruneau Meadows (see site 18), drive twenty miles north to reach Bear Creek Summit. The road winds through aspen and fir, home to western tanagers, dusky flycatchers, warbling vireos, and many other birds. Northern goshawks often fly low near aspen thickets; golden eagles ride thermal currents near rocky escarpments past Camp Draw. Before Copper Mountain summit, watch for spotted frogs and beaver lodges in ponds. Patches of mountain mahogany and squaw carpet attract mule deer and white-tailed jackrabbits. Uinta chipmunks, golden-mantled ground squirrels, northern flickers, and hairy woodpeckers inhabit the conifers. Watch for sage grouse and chukar broods on lower slopes in the summer.

Viewing Information: View while driving or from pull-outs between July 1 and September 15 only. Patience and binoculars yield best results. NARROW, STEEP GRAVEL ROAD WITH GREATER THAN 15 PERCENT GRADE (VIA JARBIDGE); NOT SUITABLE FOR CAMP TRAILERS OR MOTOR HOMES. VERY REMOTE SITE. BRING MAP, FUEL, FOOD, WATER—ESPECIALLY IF ALSO PLANNING TO SEE SITES 18 AND 20.

Directions: From Elko, drive fifty-five miles north on SR 225. Turn right (east) on CR 746 (gravel) and drive twenty-seven miles to Charleston Reservoir. Continue north on CR 748 about eight miles to national forest boundary. Begin viewing here and continue thirteen miles to summit. SEE MAP OPPOSITE PAGE.

Site Manager: USFS (208) 543-4129
Size: Thirteen-mile drive
Closest Town: Jarbidge, six miles

Ravens have long been the subject of myths and legends, probably because of their glossy black plumage and habit of feeding on dead animals. Acrobatic in flight, ravens will fearlessly chase hawks and even eagles.
KEN M. JOHNS

20 JARBIDGE CANYON

Description: AUTO TOUR. This half-mile-deep river gorge is in a wilderness of high mountains, high plateaus, and rugged lava flows. The drive begins at the canyon's lower end, passes through the town of Jarbidge, and climbs to the wilderness boundary where a trail leads to Jarbidge Lake. Look for mule deer, golden-mantled ground squirrels, least chipmunks, and rabbits in the canyon. Yellow-bellied marmots often sun themselves on boulders. Sharp-shinned hawks, golden eagles, and other birds of prey soar near canyon walls. The Jarbidge River is home to rare redband trout and the state's only population of bull trout. Forests south of the town attract many birds, including blue grouse, woodpeckers, and nuthatches. Use binoculars to spot MacGillivray's warblers, yellow-breasted chats, and other warblers along the riparian corridor.

Viewing Information: Very good year-round viewing of deer (early morning, evening), small mammals, birds of prey, and fish. Excellent songbird viewing spring through fall. Wildflowers, insects, and reptiles best seen in summer and early fall. Primitive USFS campgrounds along river. MANY RATTLESNAKES NORTH OF TOWN. ROAD MAY BE CLOSED IN WINTER, SPRING. CALL FOR INFORMATION.

Directions: *From Rogerson, Idaho, on US Highway 93, turn west toward Three Creek and drive fifty-five miles on paved and gravel roads to state line. Begin tour, drive eight miles to Jarbidge, then four miles to wilderness boundary.* SEE MAP.

Site Manager: USFS, BLM (208) 543-4129
Size: Twelve-mile drive
Closest Town: Jarbidge

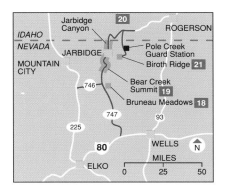

From its headwaters in a wilderness of peaks, plateaus, and forests, the Jarbidge River flows down canyon and through a deep gorge flanked by cliffs and conifer-clad slopes. Wildlife is seasonally abundant but this viewing site is extremely remote: allow plenty of time and come prepared.
PETE BRADLEY

21 BIROTH RIDGE

Description: Exceptionally remote and scenic, this five-mile hike follows the spine of 8,000-foot Biroth Ridge. Conifer forests cloak the first half of the trail; watch here for blue grouse and many finches, warblers, and woodpeckers. Look for Rocky Mountain elk on the slopes above Slide Creek. Mule deer and elk often bed down in the firs during the day. From the ridge, view the East Fork of the Jarbidge River, lofty mountain peaks, and patches of aspen and mountain brush. Use binoculars to spot northern goshawks, prairie falcons, American kestrels, and golden eagles in flight. Red-tailed hawks and golden eagles often roost and hunt from tall snags. The second half of the trail descends through grasslands, mountain mahogany, and sagebrush used by sage grouse, coyotes, deer, and elk. On the drive to Pole Creek, watch open areas for herds of pronghorn.

Viewing Information: Good viewing of elk, deer, and pronghorn from spring through fall. Plentiful songbirds and wildflowers spring and summer. Birds of prey are common in summer. Sage grouse best seen in summer and fall. Some viewing from parking area overlook. Use binoculars. NO FACILITIES. TAKE ADEQUATE FUEL, FOOD, WATER. VERY STEEP HIKING. SNOWMOBILE ACCESS ONLY IN WINTER.

Directions: From Rogerson, Idaho, take road to Three Creek west for thirty-eight miles to Pole Creek Guard Station turnoff. Turn south, toward Pole Creek, and drive nine miles. Road becomes FR 074 at national forest boundary. Continue five miles and turn south at Pole Creek Guard Station turn-off. Drive one mile south past station, turn west for one mile, then turn south .5 miles. SEE MAP.

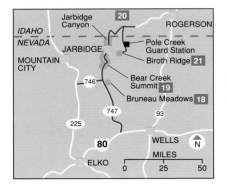

Site Manager: USFS (208) 543-4129
Size: Five-mile hike
Closest Town: Rogerson, ID, fifty-five miles

Pronghorn have a clear view of predators in Nevada's treeless landscape—habitat where North America's fastest land mammal can use its great speed and extraordinary vision to full advantage. When pronghorn flee, the long white hairs on their rumps stand erect, creating a moving white warning flag that can be seen by other pronghorn several miles away. GARY KRAMER

22 CABIN FIELD

Description: AUTO TOUR. This seven-mile stretch of the Mary's River floodplain is a wetland oasis that attracts northern pintails, cinnamon and green-winged teal, Canada geese, and other waterfowl; several species nest here. Willets, long-billed curlews, and many other shorebirds feed in the shallows. American bitterns, soras, common yellowthroats, and marsh wrens inhabit bulrush and cattails, while greater sandhill cranes, white-faced ibis, and herons are conspicuous. In willows and hay meadows, watch for mule deer and scores of songbirds, including lazuli buntings, bobolinks, and yellow-breasted chats. Western terrestrial garter snakes and leopard frogs abound. During the summer, look for sage grouse and their chicks feeding in the meadows; muskrats may also be visible. Lucky winter visitors may spot beavers, river otters, minks, and porcupines. The surrounding hills attract mule deer, pronghorn, sage thrashers, and loggerhead shrikes. Birds of prey include northern harriers, American kestrels, and wintering bald eagles.

Viewing Information: Outstanding car viewing from overlooks; use binoculars for best results. Excellent viewing of birds, reptiles, and wildflowers spring and summer. Many nesting species. Some winter songbirds. Most small mammals are common year-round. Mule deer and pronghorn easily seen spring through fall. Watch for coyotes and badgers. DIRT ROAD; VERY SLIPPERY WHEN WET. PLEASE CLOSE GATES TO KEEP COWS OFF WETLAND. PLEASE DO NOT ENTER POSTED PRIVATE RANCH PROPERTY.

Directions: *From Wells, drive west on Interstate 80 eighteen miles and take Exit 333 (Deeth). Just past town, turn north toward Charleston. Drive 8.5 miles, then turn east at the Mala Vista Ranch sign. Drive 1.5 miles and begin viewing on east side of road. End viewing at ranch boundary. SEE MAP.*

Site Manager: BLM (702) 753-0200
Size: Seven-mile drive
Closest Town: Wells, twenty-eight miles

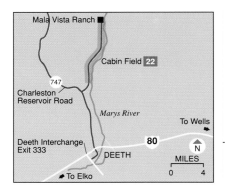

23 ANGEL LAKE

Description: Snowmelt waterfalls cascade from the sheer rock ledges that surround this cirque basin subalpine lake. Mountain goats and Rocky Mountain bighorn sheep balance on rock ledges, with bighorns occasionally visible on the road or in the campground. Look for crow-sized Clark's nutcrackers, yellow warblers, and other songbirds in the scattered pines and aspens; blue grouse and hermit thrushes may be spotted in brushy areas. In the spring and summer, painted lady butterflies flutter among meadow wildflowers. Mule deer browse in open areas, never far from cover. Red-tailed hawks and golden eagles are common.

Viewing Information: Very good viewing of bighorns and mountain goats spring through fall. Good viewing of birds of prey, songbirds, and grouse spring and summer. Butterflies and wildflowers abundant in spring and summer. Paved drive to lake very scenic; watch for wildlife. Fee camping. Barrier-free access facilities. LATE SPRING/ EARLY FALL SNOW. LAST FOUR MILES OF DRIVE ARE STEEP, WINDING. NO TRAILERS OR LARGE RVs.

Directions: *From Wells and Interstate 80, take West Wells exit to SR 231. Drive south twelve miles to site.* SEE MAP.

Site Manager: USFS (702) 752-3357
Size: 400 acres
Closest Town: Wells, twelve miles

Look beneath the eye of the Clark's nutcracker to spot its cheek pouch bulging with seeds or nuts. These crow-sized birds associated with conifer forests bury thousands of seeds in summer and fall, then visit these caches all winter long.
WILLIAM GRENFELL

Pika

Great Basin Landscapes: The Subalpine Zone

The Great Basin's water cycle often begins two miles high, in the steep mountains of the subalpine zone. As clouds move over these towering sentinels, they leave a mantle of snow over jagged rocks, sparse grasses, and wind-ravaged conifers. Runoff from melting snow or summer storms courses downslope through a streamside corridor and eventually recharges dry playa lake beds below.

Sapphire lakes abound and gnarled Great Basin bristlecone pines persist in the subalpine region—a place where winter may last ten months and spring finally arrives in July. The growing season here is extremely short and stunted plants or trees are the norm; a six-inch shrub may be more than forty years old.

The ancient bristlecone pines are living proof that "adversity begets longevity." Howling winds and savage storms may prune off large branches and strip away part of the bark, but the tree endures. Some bristlecone pines are more than 4,500 years old—the oldest living trees on earth.

The twisted forms of whitebark and limber pines also appear on the talus and granite slopes of the subalpine zone. Several species of wildlife survive and seasonally thrive in this sometimes harsh, high-elevation zone.

Wind-polished branches serve as perches for ravens, Clark's nutcrackers, and many songbirds. The birds are joined by pikas, golden-mantled ground squirrels, and other small mammals that feed on pine seeds. While few birds remain through the long winters, badgers, ground squirrels, and other excavators dig miles of underground tunnels beneath the surface and wait out the cold weather. Pikas prepare for winter by cutting summer grass and storing it, like hay, near their burrows.

When the snow melts, rugged sideslopes mantled with forbs and grasses become a summer home for bighorn sheep, mountain goats, mule deer, and elk. Wildflower-strewn wet meadows are also a veritable wildlife oasis, attracting everything from ground squirrels and mule deer to hummingbirds.

24 LAMOILLE CANYON NATIONAL SCENIC BYWAY

Description: AUTO TOUR. This rock-walled canyon features spectacular hanging valleys and alpine lakes. Look for mountain goats and Rocky Mountain bighorn sheep on high rock ledges. Scan canyon wall crevices for the nests of canyon wrens and violet-green swallows. Limber pines and aspens on the south slopes attract Uinta chipmunks, Clark's nutcrackers, blue grouse, and songbirds. North slope rocks reveal yellow-bellied marmots or pikas. Mule deer often feed or bed among the aspens. Prairie falcons, golden eagles, and other birds of prey soar aloft. Creeks and springs bordered by meadows and aspens, attract American dippers, lazuli buntings, warblers, and other birds. Take the .25-mile Changing Canyon Trail, a guided walk that explains the canyon's formation and leads to active beaver colonies. Hardy hikers may want to visit 9,600-foot Island Lake. Mountain goats, bighorn sheep, Himalayan snow cocks, and other birds may be seen near this sapphire pool.

Viewing Information: Excellent viewing from camps, picnic areas, trails on route. Very good chance of seeing deer, mountain goats, bighorn sheep, small mammals, birds of prey, and songbirds spring through fall. Many beaver ponds and occasional daytime beaver sightings. Facilities at Thomas Campground, fee camping. ROAD NOT PLOWED IN WINTER. SNOW, AVALANCHE DANGER AFTER STORMS. MUD SLIDES AFTER HEAVY RAIN.

Directions: SEE MAP OPPOSITE PAGE.

Site Manager: USFS (702) 752-3357
Size: twelve-mile drive
Closest Town: Elko, eighteen miles

Fall cloaks Lamoille Canyon in brilliant hues of crimson and gold. From its high elevation aspen groves and willow-lined streams to its mountain mahogany and pinyon-juniper uplands, this stunning scenery provides richly for wildlife.
BOB GOODMAN

25 RUBY CREST NATIONAL RECREATIONAL TRAIL

Description: Explore rugged backcountry wilderness on this forty-mile trail through high-elevation forest and tundra. The trail skirts glaciated canyons and ten alpine lakes, weaving through conifers where lazuli buntings, blue grouse, Clark's nutcrackers, and mule deer hide. It then climbs steeply into a cirque basin, and crosses aspen and willow-bordered creeks that shelter MacGillivray's warblers, Cassin's finches, and western tanagers. On the crest, watch for Himalayan snow cocks roosting on vertical talus slopes or foraging on tundra meadows. Golden eagles and red-tailed hawks scan the slopes for pikas, Uinta chipmunks, and yellow-bellied marmots. Steep ridges surrounding lakes are home to mountain goats and Rocky Mountain bighorn sheep.

Viewing Information: Excellent viewing of all featured species spring through fall. Trail usually open by July 1. Facilities at trailhead. Fee camping at Thomas Campground. Horse facilities and challenging horse trails. NO MOTORIZED VEHICLES. RUGGED BACKPACKING; GOOD PHYSICAL CONDITION REQUIRED. UP TO TEN MILES WITH NO WATER AVAILABLE. BE PREPARED FOR AUGUST SNOW. SUMMER LIGHTNING/STORMS.

Directions: From Elko, take SR 227 south eighteen miles to Lamoille Canyon Scenic Byway. Turn south and drive twelve miles to Road's End recreation site. See map for southern access. SEE MAP.

Site Manager: USFS (702) 752-3357
Size: Forty-mile-long trail
Closest Town: Elko, thirty miles

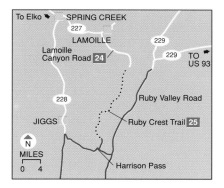

Rocky and snow-bound much of the year, the Ruby Crest Trail explores wild subalpine habitat that looks inhospitable but actually supports abundant wildlife during the summer months.
JACK WILBURN

26 RUBY LAKE NATIONAL WILDLIFE REFUGE

Description: The spring-fed marshes and wet meadows of this high-elevation valley are flanked by sagebrush uplands and the rugged Ruby Mountains. Water-associated birds are common throughout the year, including tens of thousands of migratory waterfowl in fall. More than a dozen species of ducks nest at the South and North Sumps, including thousands of canvasbacks, gadwalls, and cinnamon teal. Hundreds of nesting white-faced ibises may be seen at the South Sump, with mixed colonies of double-crested cormorants and great egrets nesting in Unit 14. Trumpeter swans, greater sandhill cranes, American coots, and several species of shorebirds, grebes, and herons also nest here. Cave Creek's riparian border offers outstanding birding year-round. Dozens of songbirds nest on or near the refuge, including hummingbirds, flycatchers, swallows, wrens, warblers, sparrows, blackbirds, and finches. The sagebrush and pinyon/juniper uplands are no less productive, drawing sage grouse, western bluebirds, and mountain chickadees. Watch overhead for golden eagles, northern harriers, American kestrels, short-eared owls, and rough-legged hawks. Many mammals are also conspicuous, including Townsend's ground squirrels, muskrats, mountain cottontails, coyotes, and mule deer.

Viewing Information: More than 200 bird species, including more than 130 known to nest locally. Fifty wintering bird species. Waterfowl nesting May through July; peak fall migration in September and October. Trumpeter swans and bald eagles are best seen late fall and winter. Excellent views of ducks, birds of prey, coyotes year round. Songbirds, shorebirds, and wading birds are abundant spring through fall; mule deer may also be seen then. Wildflowers peak in spring and summer. Eight fish species. Check boating regulations. USFS campgrounds nearby. HARRISON PASS CLOSED IN WINTER AND SNOW ON OTHER ROADS. SUMMER LIGHTNING/THUNDERSTORMS.

Directions: SEE MAP.

Site Manager: USFWS (702) 779-2237
Size: 37,632 acres
Closest Town: Elko, sixty-six miles

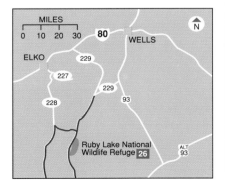

The Ruby Mountains provide a scenic backdrop for the sprawling marshes at Ruby Lake National Wildlife Refuge. This lush wetland complex attracts thousands of waterfowl and shorebirds during the fall; many species remain to nest in the spring. KENNETH L. MILLER

27 GOSHUTE MOUNTAINS

Description: Up to 20,000 birds of prey follow the Goshute Mountains' 9,000-foot ridgeline every fall, one of the largest raptor flyways in western North America. Eighteen species have been counted here. Cooper's and sharp-shinned hawks are abundant. Golden and bald eagles, northern goshawks, American kestrels, prairie and peregrine falcons, turkey vultures, and ospreys, as well as red-tailed, Swainson's, ferruginous, red-shouldered, and rough-legged hawks are also common. Hawkwatch International provides seasonal interpretive services and performs surveys, captures, and bird banding. Follow the raptor-shaped signs on the steep, two-mile hike to the observation point.

Viewing Information: SEASONAL SITE. View from mid-August to mid-October only. Hike-in viewing only. Trail climbs 1,600 feet in two miles. Wendover Welcome Center has site updates. CALL BEFORE MAKING TRIP; OCCASIONAL ACCESS RESTRICTIONS. UNMAINTAINED DIRT ROADS MAY BE IMPASSABLE WHEN WET. SUGGEST HIGH CLEARANCE VEHICLE. NO MOTORIZED VEHICLES BEYOND TRAILHEAD. TREACHEROUS CLIFFS NEAR LOOKOUT. EXTREME COLD IN LATE FALL. NO PETS, PLEASE.

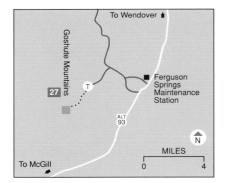

Directions: SEE MAP.

Site Manager: BLM (702) 753-0200
Size: Five acres
Closest Town: Wendover, twenty-seven miles

Thousands of birds of prey follow the Goshute Mountains ridgeline during fall migration. Members of Hawkwatch International monitor their migration trends and also offer educational programs at the mountain observation point.
ROBERT KRUIDENIER

REGION THREE:
PONY EXPRESS TERRITORY

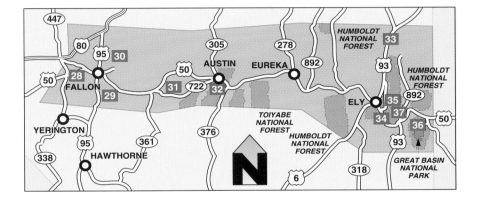

WILDLIFE VIEWING SITES
28 Lahontan State Recreation Area
29 Carson Lake
30 Stillwater National Wildlife Refuge
31 Big Den Creek
32 Kingston Canyon
33 Steptoe Valley
34 Ely Elk Viewing Site
35 Success Summit
36 Great Basin National Park
37 Cleve Creek

28 LAHONTAN STATE RECREATION AREA

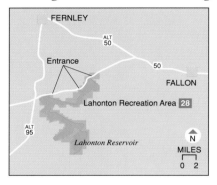

Description: Explore the cottonwood forest above Lahontan Reservoir for nothern orioles, black-headed arosbeaks, and yellow-billed cuckoos, also monarch and swallowtail butterflies. Reservoir waters near shore produce good views of Canada geese, tundra swans, and many ducks in spring. One nesting island is inhabited by ring-billed gulls and another, by California gulls. Other islands shelter nesting great blue herons. The dam site attracts common egrets, white pelicans, double-crested cormorants, western grebes, and wintering bald eagles. The surrounding sagebrush flats harbor lizards, snakes, and black-tailed jackrabbits—prey for northern harriers, great horned owls, and other birds of prey. The lower Carson River, below dam, also offers wildlife viewing.

Viewing Information: Boat and shoreline viewing. Good to excellent viewing of songbirds, gulls, butterflies, lizards, and deer from spring to fall. Look for wading birds late summer through winter. Waterfowl, birds of prey, and coyotes highly visible year-round. SANDY BEACHES; STAY ON ROADS. BE CAUTIOUS AT DAM SITE.

Directions: SEE MAP.

Site Manager: NDSP (702) 867-3500
Size: 30,362 acres
Closest Town: Fallon, eighteen miles

Lahontan State Recreation Area's abundant fishery attracts Nevada's largest concentration of wintering bald eagles. Bald eagles usually roost and hunt from shoreline trees. A variety of waterfowl and wading birds may also be seen here.
CHASE SWIFT

Description: Considered one of the Pacific Flyway's best birding spots, this shallow lake's extensive marshes offer views of tens of thousands of birds. View from dike roads and three viewing towers. Up to 15,000 snow geese stop over during spring and fall. Also common are great blue herons, and great and cattle egrets. Scores of ducks nest here; cinnamon teal nest along the shore while redheads and ruddy ducks nest on marsh vegetation, even atop muskrat lodges. The lake supports one of North America's largest white-faced ibis nesting colonies. So many shorebirds visit the Lahontan Valley that it has been designated a Western Hemisphere Shorebird Reserve. American avocets, long-billed dowitchers, Wilson's and red-necked phalaropes, and others are joined by such accidentals as Baird's sandpipers. Black terns stop over briefly in August. Yellow-headed blackbirds and marsh wrens nest among the lush vegetation, and five types of swallows can be spotted here. These large bird populations draw resident northern harriers and prairie falcons; short-eared owls, peregrine falcons, and bald eagles appear seasonally.

Viewing Information: About 100 bird species and thousands of birds. Driving tour. Excellent viewing of wading birds and shorebirds spring through fall. Excellent viewing of songbirds, waterfowl, muskrats, and coyotes all year. Snow geese are best seen mid-January to mid-March, and October to early December. Look for Canada geese in July. Best viewing for ducks March through September. White-faced ibis numbers can exceed 4,000 pairs. Look for peregrine falcons in winter and spring; bald eagles visit in winter. NO OFF-ROAD DRIVING. ROADS, DIKES MUDDY AND SLIPPERY WHEN WET. PLEASE, NO HIKING OR WADING OFF DIKES.

Directions: *From Fallon, take US Highway 95 eight miles south and turn left on Pasture Road. Drive east two miles to Greenhead Hunting Club. Gate on right; sign in at clubhouse. SEE MAP.*

Site Manager: Truckee-Carson Irrigation District (702) 423-3071
Size: 22,000 acres
Closest Town: Fallon, ten miles

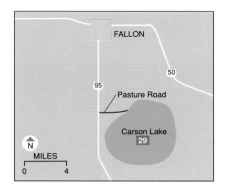

30 STILLWATER NATIONAL WILDLIFE REFUGE

Description: Nevada's largest bald eagle wintering site is also a spectacular wetland that attracts more than 250,000 waterfowl. Half of the Pacific Flyway's canvasback population gathers on ponds amidst white pelicans, tundra swans, Canada geese, and various ducks. The mudflats attract concentrations of long-billed dowitchers, American avocets, black-necked stilts, and other shorebirds. Wading birds are common. Look for prairie falcons, red-tailed hawks, northern harriers, and golden eagles near Hunter Road. Timber Lake's cottonwoods host warblers, vireos and other songbirds. Mule deer, badgers, coyotes, and kit foxes move between the desert and wetlands. Greasewood shelters loggerhead shrikes, kangaroo rats, and collared lizards.

Viewing Information: More than 160 bird species. Good car viewing. Exceptional viewing of waterfowl and wading birds spring through fall. See waterfowl best late fall. Tundra swans are best seen in early winter; pelicans, March to November. Shorebirds excellent late-April to mid-May and mid-July to late-August. See birds of prey, deer in fall and winter. Refuge a part of the 200,000-acre Stillwater WMA. NO VEHICLES ALLOWED IN REFUGE; HIKING ONLY. ROADS MUDDY WHEN WET. Headquarters in Fallon, 960-4 Auction Road.

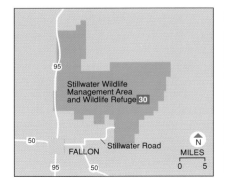

Directions: SEE MAP.

Site Manager: USFWS (702) 423-5128
Size: 77,500 acres
Closest Town: Fallon, sixteen miles

Alkali flats, beaches, and wetland shallows are a beacon for long-billed dowitchers and thousands of other shorebirds that visit the Lahontan Valley each year. Stillwater Refuge is so important to migratory shorebirds that the site has been named a Western Hemisphere Shorebird Reserve.

CLAIR KOFOED

Description: Big Den Creek slices through a slender, steep-walled canyon located in a pinyon/juniper woodland. Narrow footholds on the canyon wall may be occupied by desert bighorn sheep. The woodland, sagebrush, mountain shrub, and streamside vegetation provide multi-leveled habitats for many species. Watch for Belding's ground squirrels, mountain cottontails, least chipmunks, and bushy-tailed woodrats in the heavy underbrush. Trees attract pinyon jays, western bluebirds, green-tailed towhees, and black-headed grosbeaks. Badgers and coyotes may appear in open areas. The skies are scribed by golden eagles, prairie falcons, and American kestrels. White-throated swifts inhabit the narrow canyon that leads to the basin at the head of Big Den Creek.

Viewing Information: Good viewing of all featured species spring through fall. Spring wildflowers. Fencing minimizes livestock grazing along creek. NO FACILITIES. INACCESSIBLE AFTER HEAVY RAIN OR SNOW. HIKE IN INVOLVES DIFFICULT, ROCKY TRAIL. RATTLESNAKES COMMON.

Directions: From Fallon, drive east on US Highway 50 for forty-eight miles. At milepost 71, turn onto SR 722 and continue east about six miles. Turn east on unmarked dirt road; drive .75 mile. Take north fork 2.25 miles to exclosure. Trailhead at road's end. SEE MAP.

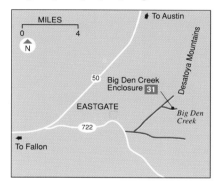

Site Manager: BLM (702) 885-6000
Size: 1,500 acres
Closest Town: Fallon, fifty-seven miles

Kit foxes are the smallest of Nevada's wild canids and are preyed on by their coyote cousins. They compete for the same rabbits, ground squirrels, and rodents.

C. ALLAN MORGAN

32 KINGSTON CANYON

Description: AUTO TOUR. Kingston Canyon's cottonwood- and willow-lined creek, wet meadow, and small lake sit in the shadow of rugged Bunker Hill. The road follows a riparian corridor, where pull-outs offer opportunities to spot warblers, vireos, sparrows, and other songbirds. The upper canyon winds through higher-elevation habitat favored by broad-tailed hummingbirds and tree swallows. Birds of prey soar near cliffs or over the wet meadow. Mule deer browse in the meadow or upslope vegetation. Side canyons attract sage thrashers; the pinyon-juniper woodland shelters mountain bluebirds, nuthatches, wrens, and towhees. The creek broadens into a small reservoir occasionally populated by waterfowl. Watch along the stream for American dippers, and belted kingfishers, and bank swallows..

Viewing Information: Good viewing of all featured wildlife between spring and fall. Watch shale cliffs along drive for deer and mountain lions during early morning, evening. Use binoculars or a spotting scope for best results. More viewing over summit at Big Creek. Fee camping and trailer parking at Kingston Campground.

Directions: *From Austin, drive east twelve miles on US Highway 50 to SR 376. Turn south and drive twenty-two miles. Turn west on FR 002 and drive three miles to end of pavement and beginning of driving tour.* SEE MAP.

Site Manager: USFS (702) 964-2671
Size: Seven-mile drive
Closest Town: Austin, thirty-seven miles

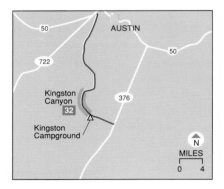

Look among the conifers for the red-breasted nuthatch as it moves up and down the trunk, using its sharp, chisel-like bill to probe under tree bark. This small, stout bird can be spotted moving quickly from tree to tree.
SCOTT PRICE

33 STEPTOE VALLEY

Description: AUTO TOUR. This drive along US Highway 93 contours the west slope of the Schell Creek Range, a prime winter viewing area for pronghorn. Pull-outs along the road offer excellent opportunities to see 250 to 300 pronghorn feeding and resting among the sagebrush and whitesage that dot the valley to the west. The pronghorns' tawny coats blend with the surroundings, but they have prominent white neck markings and large white rump patches. Watch for occasional mule deer, coyotes, horned larks, and ravens. Other winter visitors include golden eagles and rough-legged hawks.

Viewing Information: Excellent viewing for pronghorn fall through spring, all day, with peak numbers in winter. Prime viewing mornings and late afternoons. Pronghorn observed most often on west side of highway. Binoculars or a spotting scope allow close-up views. Interpretive display, facilities at Schellbourne. USE CAUTION WHEN PULLING OFF HIGHWAY TO VIEW.

Directions: *Drive-by viewing begins on US Highway 93 seven miles north of McGill, near Duck Creek turnoff, and ends five miles north of Cherry Creek turnoff.* SEE MAP.

Site Manager: BLM (702) 289-4865
Size: Thirty-three-mile drive
Closest Town: McGill, seven miles

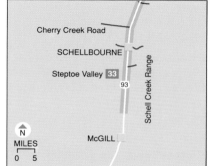

In spring this strutting male sage grouse, with chest sacs inflated, joins hundreds of others in search of a mate. The distinctive popping and burbling noises they make come from inflating and deflating their air sacs.
WILLIAM H. MULLINS

34 ELY ELK VIEWING SITE

Description: AUTO TOUR. Beginning in fall, herds of Rocky Mountain elk move from high elevation summer habitat in the Schell Creek Range to the sagebrush and grasslands bordering this nine-mile stretch of US Highway 93. Some days, 200 to 300 elk can be seen grazing within sight of the highway. Golden eagles, and ferruginous and rough-legged hawks perch on the utility lines along the road.

Viewing Information: Excellent drive-by elk viewing fall through spring; peak viewing winter and early spring. Two parking areas are connected by a one-mile road separate from highway. Best viewing at dawn and dusk. On cold, clear, windless days, elk may be visible all day. During fall and early winter, bulls have large antlers. Each year, they shed their antlers in late winter/early spring and usually grow a new, larger set during summer. Birds of prey present summer and fall; ferruginous hawks in summer. PLEASE PULL INTO PARKING AREAS TO VIEW. FACILITIES AT CAVE LAKE STATE PARK, FIVE MILES TO EAST.

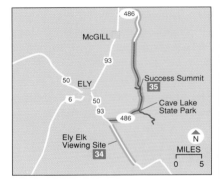

Directions: *Drive-by viewing along US Highway 93, beginning six miles south of Ely and ending fifteen miles south of Ely.* SEE MAP.

Site Manager: BLM (702) 289-4865
Size: Nine-mile drive
Closest Town: Ely, six miles

Drive-by viewing of Rocky Mountain elk is nothing less than spectacular on this stretch of highway south of Ely. During fall, be sure to listen for an eerie chorus of squeals and grunts— the sounds of bull elk "bugling" during the fall rut.
MICHAEL S. SAMPLE

58

35 SUCCESS SUMMIT

Description and Directions: AUTO TOUR. This drive traverses many habitats, including sagebrush flats and an emerald lake bounded by sheer cliffs. From Ely, travel south on US Highway 93, passing through several sagebrush benches, watching for mule deer, black-tailed jackrabbits, least chipmunks, sage grouse, and coyotes. Turn east on CR 486 to parallel the riparian border of Steptoe Creek—the leafy canopy often shelters yellow warblers, dark-eyed juncos, and other songbirds. Golden eagles and prairie falcons roost and nest in limestone cliffs and rock outcroppings between here and Water Canyon. Ferruginous hawks and northern harriers are also common. Spend time exploring Cave Lake State Park, where a five-mile interpretive trail offers chances to see migratory birds and mammals. Resume the drive, climbing toward 8,950-foot Success Summit. Many small herds of Rocky Mountain elk feed on the open sagebrush hillsides, close to cover, during the summer. Blue grouse inhabit the conifers, as do secretive hermit thrushes and brown creepers. Look among the aspens at Water Canyon and other riparian areas for woodpeckers, yellow-rumped and Wilson's warblers, and warbling and solitary vireos. These areas also shelter fawns during summer. The road gradually descends through Duck Creek Basin, then rejoins US Highway 93. SEE MAP OPPOSITE PAGE.

Viewing Information: Excellent viewing of elk, mule deer, and sage grouse spring through fall. Watch for elk early morning, late evening. Small mammals and coyotes may be spotted year round. Good views of birds of prey, songbirds, water-associated birds, and wildflowers spring through fall. Mountain lions and bobcats common but nocturnal. Facilities at Cave Lake; also fees and boating restrictions. ROAD BEYOND PARK REQUIRES HIGH-CLEARANCE VEHICLE AND IS IMPASSABLE WHEN WET. CLOSED IN WINTER.

Site Manager: USFS, BLM, NDSP (702) 289-3031
Size: Thirty-three-mile drive
Closest Town: Ely, seven miles

MacGillivray's warbler

Great Basin Landscapes: The Riparian Zone

Vegetation-lined streams meander down Nevada's mountain slopes, linking subalpine zones with the dry desert below. These small creeks and rivers, with their associated vegetation, are called riparian corridors. They are the lifeblood of the Great Basin Desert.

It's easy to identify riparian corridors. Just watch for a lush band of tall trees, low-lying shrubs, and grasses growing along the banks of a river or stream. This network of plantlife forms an ideal environment for a wide variety of wildlife, providing food, water, shelter, and hidden pathways for travel.

Streamside trees are home to squirrels, woodpeckers, and migratory songbirds. Low-lying shrubs often conceal ground-dwelling birds, small mammals, and reptiles. Some streams pass through canyons with sheer rock walls, where swifts, swallows, and birds of prey make their nests. Bighorn sheep rest of rock ledges near the water.

Mountain lions, bobcats, and other secretive animals spend at least part of their time in the riparian corridor—look along stream banks for their tracks. Otters leave well-worn slide marks along the bank; beavers build dams across streams. Many species of fish live in Great Basin waterways, including some that are endangered.

Many animals that rely on the riparian corridor actually live in the sagebrush steppe area nearby. These open sideslopes and plains support nearly half of the Great Basin's plant species.

36 ⬛ GREAT BASIN NATIONAL PARK

Description: From high desert sagebrush to Lehman Cave's colorful formations, from bristlecone pines to Wheeler Peak's alpine lakes, this park offers stunning scenery and abundant wildlife. Look for cliff chipmunks near the visitor center and mule deer in the adjacent meadow. Stop at Baker Creek Campground, where yellow-bellied marmots pass the summer near camp. Hike the Baker and Lehman Creek trails, keeping a watch for mule deer, American dippers, and swallowtail butterflies. Aspen corridors shelter red-naped sapsuckers. At dawn or in the evening, watch for gray fox, bobcat, or mountain lion. Pinyon pines attract crows, pinyon jays, and Clark's nutcrackers. Take the Wheeler Peak Scenic Drive to see mule deer, coyotes, black-tailed jackrabbits, and striped skunks near the road. Golden eagles, prairie falcons, and sharp-shinned hawks are common. Campground trails lead to alpine lakes mantled with bristlecone pines—the oldest living trees on earth. Trailside trees shelter thrushes, chickadees, juncos, warblers, and jays. Visit Snake Creek Canyon to see yellow-rumped warblers, warbling vireos, chipping sparrows, red crossbills, brown creepers, Steller's jays, and similar species.

Viewing Information: Very good viewing of deer and jays year-round. Excellent songbird viewing spring through fall. Good views of birds of prey, small mammals, carnivores spring through fall. Butterflies and wildflowers appear in spring and summer. Some car viewing. Many animal tracks near visitor center. Fee camping. PLEASE PULL OFF ROAD WHEN VIEWING. ROAD TO WHEELER PEAK CAMPGROUND IS NARROW, STEEP, WITH MANY CURVES. MANY HIKES ARE STEEP, STRENUOUS, HIGH ELEVATION. SUMMER TRAFFIC CAN BE HEAVY.

Directions: *From US Highway 50 and Nevada border, travel west seven miles to SR 487. Turn south and drive five miles to SR 488; turn west and drive five miles to visitor center.* SEE MAP.

Site Manager: NPS (702) 234-7331
Size: 77,100 acres
Closest Town: Baker, five miles

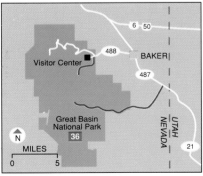

Nevada's only national park preserves the grandeur and variety of the Great Basin region. From lofty Wheeler Peak to stunning Lehman Cave, Great Basin National Park offers a wealth of scenery and habitats for wildlife. JOHN P. GEORGE

37 CLEVE CREEK

Description: AUTO TOUR. Cleve Creek and its North Fork originate high in the conifer forests and rocky peaks of the Schell Creek Range. The road crosses the creek several times, winding above benches that serve as winter range for Rocky Mountain mule deer. Deer browse in forest clearings, narrow canyons, or sagebrush uplands and may often be seen right from the car. Northern flickers, hairy woodpeckers, and red-breasted nuthatches dwell in the conifers, while chickadees, bushtits, and pinyon jays inhabit the pinyon/juniper woodlands. Willows, dogwoods, and cottonwoods border the creek and hide green-tailed towhees, yellow warblers, and yellow-breasted chats. Watch the stream for American dippers. The canyon gradually broadens into uplands that shelter occasional mourning doves, common nighthawks, short-eared owls, and coyotes. Hike into the North Fork, where beaver dams have created small ponds visited occasionally by waterfowl and shorebirds during spring and summer.

Viewing Information: On the drive along SR 893, watch for bald eagles (winter), golden eagles, prairie falcons, and occasional pronghorn. Excellent car viewing with some pull-outs. Deer are present year-round, especially winter and early spring. Good songbird viewing spring through fall; to locate birds, try standing quietly for several minutes and listening. HIGH CLEARANCE VEHICLE ADVISED; NUMEROUS CREEK CROSSINGS. SNOW, ICE IN WINTER.

Directions: *From Ely, take US Highway 93 east twenty-seven miles to SR 893. Turn north and drive twelve miles, then turn west onto CR 1073, a dirt road (later called FR 435). Drive 2.75 miles to BLM campground; driving tour begins here and continues west 10.75 miles.* SEE MAP.

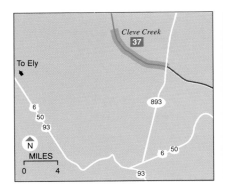

Site Manager: USFS, BLM (702) 289-3031
Size: 10.75-mile drive
Closest Town: Ely, forty-two miles

REGION FOUR: PIONEER TERRITORY

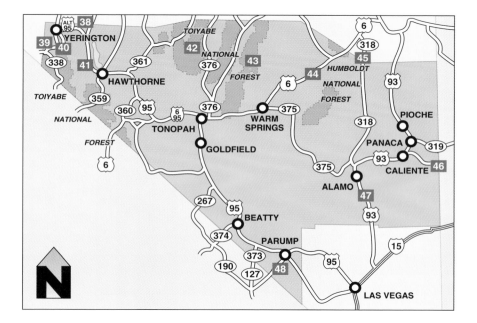

WILDLIFE VIEWING SITES
38 Mason Valley Wildlife Management Area
39 Wellington Deer Range
40 Wilson Canyon
41 Walker Lake
42 Stewart Creek
43 Table Mountain Wilderness
44 Chimney Springs
45 White River Valley
46 Beaver Dam State Park
47 Pahranagat National Wildlife Refuge
48 Ash Meadows National Wildlife Refuge

38 | MASON VALLEY WILDLIFE MANAGEMENT AREA

Description: This extensive wetland near the Walker River attracts mallards, gadwalls, redheads, white pelicans, Canada geese, and other waterfowl. Long-billed dowitchers, American avocets, and common snipe feed in the shallows. Great blue herons, white-faced ibis, and several egret species are conspicuous; American bitterns hide among shoreline vegetation. Gulls and terns are common. The wetlands are divided by levees and interspersed with Nevada's most extensive stands of buffaloberry, which provide cover and food for California quail, ring-necked pheasants, Rio Grande turkeys, and dozens of songbird species. Badgers, raccoons, porcupines, and rabbits also hide in the dense cover. Mule deer graze in open areas. Red-tailed, hawks, Swainson's hawks, great horned owls, and barn owls all nest in the area.

Viewing Information: Outstanding diversity of species. View from levees or car. Excellent viewing of deer, predators, small mammals, birds of prey, waterfowl, aquatic and upland birds year-round. Best area in Nevada to see turkeys. Songbirds, shorebirds, wading birds, reptiles, amphibians, and butterflies abundant spring through fall. Adjacent fish hatchery offers trout viewing. AREA MUDDY WHEN WET; STAY ON ROADS.

Directions: *From Yerington, take Alternate US Highway 95 north 4.5 miles to Miller Lane and turn east. Drive three miles, pass fish hatchery, and continue to wetlands.* SEE MAP.

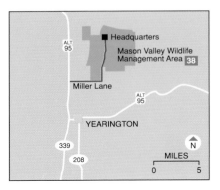

Site Manager: NDOW (702) 463-2741
Size: 12,030 acres
Closest Town: Yerington, eleven miles

Nevada's most extensive stands of buffaloberry provide excellent cover for upland birds in the Mason Valley, the best place in the state to view Rio Grande turkeys. Turkeys are wary and rarely stray far from cover.
LEONARD LEE RUE III

39 ▌**WELLINGTON DEER RANGE**

Description: AUTO TOUR. Drive through the heart of scenic Smith Valley to the mule deer winter range at Pine Nut Mountains. The range's bitterbrush, sagebrush, and juniper blanket the steep slopes on the west side of the road and serve as ideal food and cover for the deer. Hundreds can be seen at one time. Deer also use the cultivated fields on the east side of the road. Look here for other winter residents, including western meadowlarks, horned larks, ravens, and such aerial hunters as red-tailed hawks, rough-legged hawks, American kestrels, and golden eagles. Coyotes, black-tailed jackrabbits, and other songbirds may be spotted year-round.

Viewing Information: Drive-by viewing on SR 208. Best views from Upper Colony Road; numerous pull-outs. Peak viewing in winter, especially early morning and late afternoon, when deer move between cover and feeding areas. RESPECT PRIVATE PROPERTY; PLEASE DON'T CLIMB FENCES OR TRESPASS. NO FACILITIES.

Directions: From Carson City, take US Highway 395 south thirty-seven miles to Holbrook Junction. Turn east on SR 208 and drive ten miles to Upper Colony Road. Turn north; view for six miles. SEE MAP.

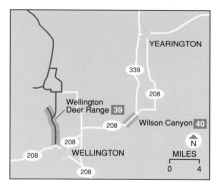

Site Manager: BLM (702) 885-6000
Size: Six-mile drive
Closest Town: Yerington, twenty-six miles

Sagebrush covers about forty percent of the state and provides for myriad species of wildlife.
DENNIS FLAHERTY

40 WILSON CANYON

Description: State Route 208 follows the West Walker River through a narrow, twisting canyon of volcanic cliffs. The sheer walls include crevices and ledges for the nests of white-throated swifts, cliff swallows, and rock wrens. Look high for the bulky stick nests of golden eagles and red-tailed hawks, and the whitewashed, pothole nests of prairie falcons. American kestrels and Cooper's hawks may occasionally be seen. American dippers appear along the stream and nest on walls and ledges near the water. MacGillivray's warblers, yellow-breasted chats, and other songbirds also nest within the riparian corridor. Watch for lizards sunning on exposed rocks.

Viewing Information: Drive-by viewing with some pull-outs. Excellent opportunities to see birds of prey, warblers, vireos, swifts, flycatchers, and other songbirds spring through fall. Facilities at west end of canyon.

Directions: *From Yerington, take Alternate US Highway 95 west one mile. Turn south on SR 339 and drive twelve miles to SR 208. Turn west and begin viewing. SEE MAP.*

Site Manager: BLM, PVT (702) 885-6000
Size: 1.5-mile drive
Closest Town: Yerington, thirteen miles

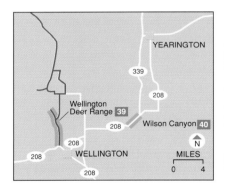

The Walker River gushes through Wilson Canyon's rocky gorge, past crevices and cliff ledges that shelter bats and cliff swallows, white-throated swifts, and American dippers.
KENNETH L. MILLER

Description: Fifteen miles long and six miles wide, this remnant of ancient Lake Lahontan is surrounded by vast expanses of desert scrub. The Walker River flows into these deep blue waters, an oasis for thousands of migratory birds, including hundreds of common loons. Snow geese, white pelicans, and several species of grebe are sometimes joined by such coastal stragglers as brants, harlequin ducks, and oldsquaws. Snowy plovers feed along the shoreline and American avocets and black-necked stilts wade in the shallows. Golden eagles and prairie falcons nest on the cliffs near Cottonwood Canyon. Whiptail and zebra-tailed lizards are common. The lake also supports threatened Lahontan cutthroat trout.

Viewing Information: Best viewing in April-May and October-November. View from boats, shoreline road, and pull-outs. Some ducks present all year. Excellent viewing of loons, grebes, pelicans, and coastal stragglers spring and fall. Shorebirds are best seen spring through fall; look for snow geese November through March. Squirrels and lizards are present spring and summer. Facilities at campgrounds. 4WD SUGGESTED FOR SANDY EAST SHORE ROADS. LAKE DANGEROUS DURING HIGH WINDS.

Directions: SEE MAP.

Site Manager: BLM (702) 885-6000
Size: Seventy square miles
Closest Town: Hawthorne, five miles

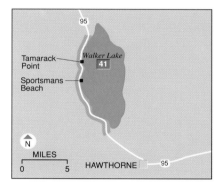

Although this western grebe appears to be alone, these gregarious diving ducks usually swim among large rafts of other grebes and waterfowl, including loons. Pairs of western grebes engage in dramatic spring courtship displays.
LEONARD LEE RUE III

69

42 STEWART CREEK

Description: The ridges and canyons of the Arc Dome Wilderness border this clear-running creek, home to Lahontan cutthroat trout. Columbine Campground offers an excellent base for viewing wildlife. A colony of Belding ground squirrels inhabit burrows near the road, a half-mile before camp and close to the horse camp and trail. Patient observers may see the colony watched and preyed upon by northern goshawks, prairie falcons, coyotes, and badgers. Cavities in the aspens belong to hairy and downy woodpeckers, northern flickers, and yellow-bellied sapsuckers. In the spring, about forty species of birds nest near camp. Hike to 11,775-foot Arc Dome and watch for sage grouse in the meadows and sagebrush and blue grouse in Nevada's largest stand of limber pines. Desert bighorn sheep, mountain lions, and bobcats inhabit the rocky, high-elevation basins.

Viewing Information: Trout visible year-round. Excellent viewing of squirrels, birds of prey, songbirds, and woodpeckers spring and summer. Good views of bighorn sheep and grouse spring through fall. Fee camping. REMOTE SITE. CARRY EXTRA FOOD, WATER, FUEL.

Directions: *From Austin, take US Highway 50 west two miles to Old US 50. Turn southwest, drive seven miles, then turn south on paved road signed "Ione, 43 miles." Road becomes gravel after five miles. Continue another thirty miles, then turn east .5 mile past Reese River Guard Station onto FS 119. Drive nine miles to Columbine Camp.* SEE MAP.

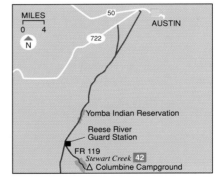

Site Manager: USFS (702) 964-2671
Size: 1,500 acres
Closest Town: Austin, fifty-three miles

Mountain lions—also called cougars, catamounts, and pumas—are closely associated with deer. They are solitary hunters and can be seen hunting during the day in unpopulated areas.
JAN L. WASSINK

Description: Hike or ride horses on more than 100 miles of trails to explore this unique Great Basin wilderness plateau flanking 10,856-foot Monitor Peak. Trails through pinyon, juniper, and mountain mahogany may flush out black-tailed jackrabbits, desert cottontails, and blue grouse. Limber pines and spectacular aspen groves shelter nuthatches, warblers, Townsend's solitaires, and fox sparrows. Wildflower-strewn meadows attract mule deer and mountain bluebirds. Golden eagles, northern goshawks, and prairie falcons glide over grasslands and meadows, important summer range of Rocky Mountain elk. Flooded areas and chewed aspens are sure signs of beaver. Sagebrush-grasslands attract sage grouse. Coyotes prowl by day; mountain lions at night.

Viewing Information: All viewing from June through mid-September. Excellent viewing of deer, elk, sage grouse, coyotes, songbirds, birds of prey, and wildflowers. Large concentrations of forest-dwelling hawks. VERY REMOTE AREA. COME PREPARED FOR WILDERNESS. NO FACILITIES.

Directions: From Tonopah, take US Highway 6 east six miles to SR 376 and turn north. Drive thirteen miles, taking turnoff to Belmont. Drive twenty-six miles to town site, then continue two miles. Turn northeast, drive four miles to Barley Creek turnoff and turn east. Drive seven miles, pass guard station, and drive another five miles to trailhead. SEE MAP.

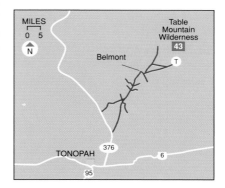

Site Manager: USFS (702) 482-6286
Size: 98,000 acres
Closest Town: Tonopah, sixty-three miles

Horned larks prefer flat, open land with low vegetation. They often walk and run on the ground, searching for insects and seeds. Watch for them throughout the state, near sagebrush and grassland-bordered roads.
JOHN GERLACH

44 CHIMNEY SPRINGS

Description: In the midst of Railroad Valley's desert, hot springs form three shallow pools and a narrow band of saltgrass wetlands. The clear, warm water sustains a threatened springfish found only in the Railroad and Duckwater valleys of Nevada. These hardy fish tolerate hot and cool water alike and, though short-lived, breed year-round. Distinct olive and yellow-green stripes on the upper body make them easy to spot in the clear water; watch them feed on insects and floating vegetation. Sandpipers and killdeer patrol the pond perimeters. Look for coyotes and kit fox scavenging among pond vegetation.

Viewing Information: Springfish viewing excellent year-round, but best early spring to late summer when males exhibit bright spawning colors. Watch for shorebirds and songbirds spring through fall; please do not disturb nesting habitat near ponds. No facilities. VERY REMOTE. WATER VERY HOT. ROUGH ROADS AND MUDDY SOILS. RECOMMEND 4WD.

Directions: *From Ely, take US Highway 6 southwest seventy-four miles to Locke's Ranch. Continue .2 mile and turn south on dirt road. Drive six miles. Knoll and fenced enclosure visible east of road; take access road .4 mile to spring.* SEE MAP.

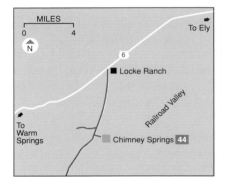

Site Manager: BLM (702) 482-7800
Size: Two acres
Closest Town: Ely, eighty-one miles

Even this seemingly barren Railroad Valley landscape supports wildlife. This is one of three shallow thermal pools inhabited by threatened springfish. Shorebirds and small mammals also visit this wetland. MARK BIDDLECOMB/BUREAU OF LAND MANAGEMENT

45 WHITE RIVER VALLEY

Description: Hay fields, grain stubble, and spring runoff are a magnet for greater sandhill cranes traveling from the lower Colorado River to northeastern Nevada nesting grounds. Cranes from this isolated population are thought to be the largest of their kind in North America. As many as 1,600 of these stately birds forage and roost on these private lands. Western meadowlarks and red-winged blackbirds fill the air with their songs, and the skies are scribed by hunting red-tailed and ferruginous hawks. Watch for occasional ring-necked pheasants among the grasses and fence rows.

Viewing Information: Excellent viewing of cranes in spring and fall, particularly between February 15 and March 15. Bring binoculars or a spotting scope to aid in viewing; keep distance from birds to avoid disturbing. Red-tailed hawks are resident, and songbirds are highly visible spring through fall. Cranes use private fields in and around Lund and Preston; their distribution changes with field use. PULL OFF ROAD TO VIEW. PRIVATE LANDS.

Directions: *South of Ely, take SR 6 southwest for twenty-two miles. Turn east on SR 318 and travel 11.7 miles to Lund. Turn at town center. From here, travel two miles west, 1.25 miles north, 1.5 miles east, then return to Lund. SEE MAP.*

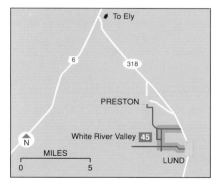

Site Manager: PVT (702) 289-1655
Size: Five square miles
Closest Town: Lund

Greater sandhill cranes ride thermal currents to and from the White River Valley every spring and fall. They assemble in large, noisy groups to feed in flooded fields on hay and grain stubble.
C. ALLAN MORGAN

46 BEAVER DAM STATE PARK

Description: In a remote corner of Nevada, stream-laced canyons, pine forests, and a small reservoir offer excellent scenery and wildlife habitat. Fallen trees and dams in the Beaver Dam Wash are clear evidence of these aquatic mammals. Great blue herons fish in the shallows. Look in the stream or overhanging trees for belted kingfishers. Streamside trees shelter warblers, hummingbirds, pinyon jays, and northern flickers. Schroeder Reservoir attracts mallards, redheads, Canada geese, and mule deer. The sagebrush understory conceals antelope ground squirrels, black-tailed jackrabbits, and occasional long-tailed weasels. Watch for soaring red-tailed hawks, golden eagles, and great horned owls. At night, lucky campers may spot beavers, ringtails, or gray foxes. Gopher and garter snakes, and Great Basin rattlesnakes are common.

Viewing Information: Good year-round viewing of deer, some predators, birds of prey, and waterfowl. Excellent viewing of small mammals, songbirds, shorebirds, wading birds, reptiles, and amphibians spring through fall. Abundant wildflowers spring and summer. Watch for bats in flight at dusk, in summer. REMOTE AREA. LIMITED BARRIER-FREE VIEWING.

Directions: SEE MAP.

Site Manager: NDSP (702) 728-4467
Size: 2,300 acres
Closest Town: Caliente, thirty-four miles

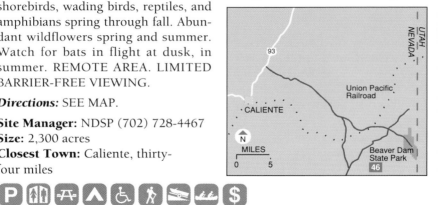

Weighing in at four to five ounces, the white-tailed antelope ground squirrel is the smallest of the ground squirrels. It copes with hotter daytime temperatures than other desert dwellers by curving its long tail over its back, like an umbrella.

DENNIS FLAHERTY

47 PAHRANAGAT NATIONAL WILDLIFE REFUGE

Description: Paiute Indians named this oasis of lakes and marshes "a place of many waters." Dikes bordering North Marsh and Upper Lake offer easy viewing. Shoreline cottonwoods attract many types of warblers, orioles, finches, and sparrows. Deep water provides habitat for double-crested cormorants, also western and Clark's grebes. Canada geese, tundra swans, and bald and golden eagles are common winter visitors. Cultivated fields attract greater sandhill cranes during spring migration. Geese, cormorants, and great blue herons nest at the north end of the refuge. Look for muskrats in the shallows, along with mallards, northern pintail, green-winged teal, and several species of egrets. Shorebirds come in all sizes, from western sandpipers to black-necked stilts. Scan the fields bordering the wetlands for western meadowlarks, mule deer, coyotes, and bobcats. The surrounding desert may yield views of mourning doves, Gambel's quail, greater roadrunners, and several reptiles. Northern harriers and other birds of prey are common.

Viewing Information: More than 200 bird species. Good year-round viewing of all featured birds and mammals. Waterfowl and songbird populations peak March, April, September, and October. Excellent viewing from car along Upper and Lower lakes. Non-motorized boats only.

Directions: SEE MAP.

Site Manager: USFWS (702) 725-3417
Size: 5,380 acres
Closest Town: Alamo, four miles

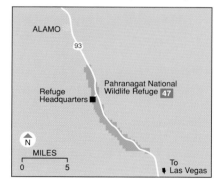

Scores of water-associated bird species rely on Pahranagat's marshes and lakes as a migratory stopover and nesting habitat. This male cinnamon teal is bright with breeding plumage.
LEN RUE JR.

75

48 | ASH MEADOWS NATIONAL WILDLIFE REFUGE

Description: Buffered by the vast Mojave desert, this spectacular desert oasis has thirty seeps, springs, and braided streams that pool into desert wetlands. The refuge safeguards habitat for twenty-six plants and animals found nowhere else on earth, including four endangered fish: the Ash Meadows speckled dace, Ash Meadows Amargosa pupfish, Warm Springs pupfish, and the Devil's Hole pupfish. Look down into Devil's Hole, a cavern pool with its own species of pupfish. Watch the Ash Meadows Amargosa pupfish dart back and forth within easy view at Crystal Pool, and in the warm water of Jackrabbit pool. Crystal and Peterson reservoirs draw canvasbacks, mallards, and redheads during the fall and winter. Many shorebird species feed in the shallows, including American avocets, Wilson's phalaropes, and dowitchers. Great blue herons and white-faced ibis appear in the marshy areas near lower Crystal Marsh. The skies above the lakes are scribed by California gulls, ring-billed gulls, and occasional black terns. Also watch for northern harriers, prairie falcons, and other birds of prey. Look toward the desert for glimpses of rabbits.

Viewing Information: Excellent viewing of fish year-round, peaking in spring when the male pupfish turn brilliant blue and vigorously defend their territories. Excellent viewing of shorebirds and wading birds winter and spring. Summer blooms of many unique plants and wildflowers. HOT SPRINGS AND HOT WATER! BRING ADEQUATE DRINKING WATER. ROADS IMPASSABLE WHEN WET.

Directions: *In Pahrump, take SR 160 north 8.5 miles to the Bell Vista Road. Turn west and drive 17.5 miles. Take right fork of gravel road and continue through refuge.* SEE MAP.

Site Manager: USFWS (702) 372-5435
Size: 23,000 acres
Closest Town: Pahrump, twenty-six miles

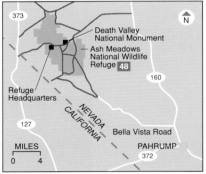

76

*Desert vegetation cloaks
Jackrabbit Spring and sedges
partially conceal this small, crystal-clear pond. Spring water constantly recharges
the pool, which supports three species of fish, including the endangered Ash
Meadows speckled dace (inset photo).* PHOTOS COURTESY U.S. FISH AND WILDLIFE SERVICE

REGION FIVE: LAS VEGAS TERRITORY

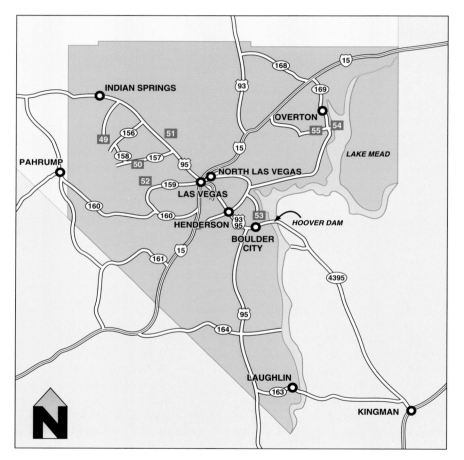

WILDLIFE VIEWING SITES
49 Bonanza Trailhead
50 Mount Charleston Loop
51 Corn Creek/Desert National Wildlife Refuge
52 Red Rock Canyon National Conservation Area
53 Black Canyon
54 Virgin River Confluence
55 Valley of Fire State Park

49 BONANZA TRAILHEAD

Description: Drive through the site of a recent 10,000-acre wildfire and see how changes in plant communities affect wildlife. The burned desert shrub plants have been replaced by perennial grasses that attract Rocky Mountain elk, mule deer, turkeys, and chukars. Coyotes, bobcats, gray foxes, and mountain lions stalk small mammals that inhabit these open grasslands. From the trailhead, take a strenuous twelve-mile hike into Lee Canyon, located in the shadow of 10,425-foot Bonanza Peak. Ponderosa and bristlecone pines provide lofty perches for hunting golden eagles, northern goshawks, and occasional peregrine falcons. Scan the needled canopy for Palmer's chipmunks, pinyon jays, scrub jays, and rufous-sided towhees. Look closely for western bluebirds, Bewick's wrens, mountain chickadees and other songbirds.

Viewing Information: Excellent viewing from car en route to trailhead; remain in vehicle for viewing. Elk, deer, and upland birds best seen at dawn and dusk, fall through spring. Use binoculars or a spotting scope. Good viewing of all other featured species throughout the year. Limited parking at trailhead. SNOW MAY CLOSE ROAD BETWEEN NOVEMBER AND FEBRUARY.

Directions: *From Las Vegas, take US Highway 95 north thirty miles to Cold Creek Road (Correctional Center turn-off). Turn west and drive thirteen miles to Willow Creek Junction and begin viewing. Pavement ends 2.5 miles before trailhead.* SEE MAP.

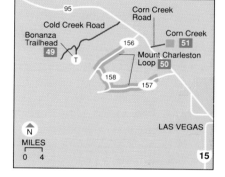

Site Manager: USFS (702) 873-8800
Size: three miles
Closest Town: Indian Springs, twenty-two miles

Nevada's most common mammal is the black-tailed jackrabbit. Adapted to the chase, its long ears move constantly to gather sounds and its powerful hind legs propel it forward in ten to twenty foot hops.
JOHN GERLACH

50 | MOUNT CHARLESTON LOOP

Description and Directions: AUTO TOUR. This viewing area, a half-hour's drive from Las Vegas, encompasses desert foothills, forested slopes, rushing streams, and rugged, 11,000-foot peaks. From Las Vegas, drive north on US Highway 95 fourteen miles to SR 157 and turn west. The drive up Kyle Canyon begins in the desert domain of collared lizards, striped whipsnakes, and other reptiles. It climbs gradually into the lower canyon, a home to sharp-shinned hawks, common nighthawks, black-throated sparrows, and occasional coyotes. Look among pinyon pines and mountain mahogany near the Guard Station for mule deer, turkeys, band-tailed pigeons, and several types of jays. Ponderosa pines cloak the canyon's upper reaches and surround Mount Charleston Lodge, providing views of Uinta chipmunks, Palmer's chipmunks, and several species of woodpeckers and hummingbirds. Listen for whip-poor-wills at the lodge parking lot. Trails lead toward Mount Charleston, where limestone cliffs and wind-ravaged bristlecone pines are a summer home to Rocky Mountain elk, flammulated owls, and many songbirds. Drive back to SR 158 and travel north, stopping at Desert View to watch soaring northern goshawks. Turn left on SR 156 to visit Lee Canyon Ski Area, a spot favored by evening grosbeaks and mountain bluebirds. Throughout the loop, rock squirrels scurry across boulders and golden-mantled ground squirrels inhabit the ponderosas. Creeks or springs harbor Pacific treefrogs, western tanagers, and many nesting birds. On the way back to US Highway 95, stop at Mack's Canyon to see Williamson's sapsuckers and rufous hummingbirds. SEE MAP BELOW.

Viewing Information: Spectacular diversity. Many trails, one barrier-free. Habitat transitions and their associated wildlife are similar on both SR 156 and SR 157. Allow at least four hours for car viewing. Small mammal and some songbird viewing year-round; excellent in spring with many nesting songbirds. Elk and deer best fall through spring. Reptiles are visible in summer. HEAVY WEEKEND TRAFFIC. PULL OFF ROAD WHEN VIEWING.

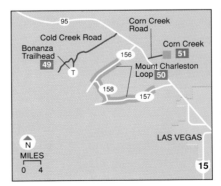

Site Manager: USFS (702) 873-8800
Size: Twenty-eight-mile drive
Closest Town: Las Vegas, thirty miles

Yellow-bellied marmots live on rocky slopes, often denning in crevices, under rocks, or within boulder-strewn hillsides. These wary mammals flee at the first hint of danger and vocalize their distress with distinctive chirps or whistles.
DAVID K. ROSEN

51 | CORN CREEK - DESERT NATIONAL WILDLIFE REFUGE

Description: This refuge, largest in the lower forty-eight states, was established to protect bighorn sheep. A major attraction is Corn Creek—ten acres of spring-fed ponds that are a birder's paradise. The pools sustain the minnow-sized Pahrump poolfish, a transplanted endangered species. Combined shoreline vegetation, pastures, and adjacent woodlands at Corn Creek attract more than 200 bird species, including dozens of nesting species and many accidentals. Yellow-rumped warblers, yellow-headed blackbirds, and phainopeplas are fairly common. Patient birders may also spot western tanagers and black-chinned hummingbirds. The desert areas offer some drive-by viewing of other wildlife. To see bighorn sheep in the summer, hike to springs or water holes. From fall to early spring, the sheep inhabit steep cliffs in the southern Sheep Mountain Range.

Viewing Information: Western half of refuge closed due to gunnery range. Excellent year-round views of bird species with peak viewing in spring. Observe fish spring through fall. Bighorns and reptiles are best seen in summer. Visitor center, facilities at Corn Creek. FOR REST OF REFUGE, 4WD VEHICLE ADVISED; VERY ROUGH ROADS. BRING FOOD, WATER, FUEL.

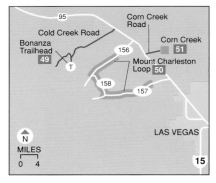

Directions: SEE MAP.

Site Manager: USFWS (702) 646-3401
Size: ten acres
Closest Town: Las Vegas, twenty-seven miles

The coloration of the zebra-tailed lizard blends readily with its sandy, gravely surroundings and provides one form of safety. This small lizard's capacity for incredible bursts of speed provides another level of protection.
JIM STAMATES

52 RED ROCK CANYON NATIONAL CONSERVATION AREA

Description: A thirteen-mile (one-way) scenic drive leads to trails, narrow canyons, sandstone cliffs, and riparian areas that attract roadrunners, rufous-sided towhees, white-throated swifts, loggerhead shrikes, and several upland birds. Clumps of vegetation shelter white-tailed antelope squirrels, black-tailed jackrabbits, and desert kangaroo rats. Look for rock squirrels and a variety of lizards on the sun-warmed rocks; be wary of poisonous snakes in shrubby, sandy areas. Red-tailed hawks, Cooper's hawks, and other birds of prey may also be watching for small animals. About 160 desert bighorn sheep inhabit the rough cliff country. They often visit water-filled basins at La Madre Spring, White Rock Spring, and Willow Spring. These basins also draw mule deer, coyotes, and mountain lions. Look for songbirds near Lost Creek's year-round spring and seasonal waterfall.

Viewing Information: Excellent wildlife diversity. More than 100 songbird species with excellent spring and fall viewing. Good viewing of bighorns, antelope ground squirrels, and birds of prey all year. Reptiles abundant. Visitor Center. Park in designated areas. Loop drive closed at night. COME PREPARED FOR SUMMER HEAT AND FLASH FLOODS. BEWARE OF ROCK-CLIMBING HAZARDS.

Directions: *From Las Vegas, take Charleston Blvd. west fifteen miles to entrance. SEE MAP.*

Site Manager: BLM (702) 363-1921
Size: 83,100 acres
Closest Town: Las Vegas, fifteen miles

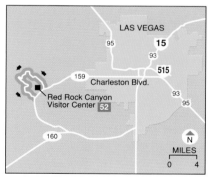

The patterned shell of the desert tortoise provides protection from predators and the elements, while its scaly, leatherlike skin shields it from thorns and barbs. The desert tortoise further copes with the desert by retaining water.
BARBARA GERLACH

53 BLACK CANYON

Description: RIVER VIEWING. Float in a raft down the Colorado River for thirteen miles, watching for wildlife along this narrow gorge. Just below Hoover Dam, look on rock ledges for the spring nests of double-crested cormorants. Secluded rock hollows provide nest sites for peregrine falcons; four pairs of these endangered birds and their fledglings inhabit the canyon. Watch the steep walls for desert bighorn sheep; some may be spotted along the river. Small cliff crevices belong to nesting white-throated swifts, rock wrens, and cliff and rough-winged swallows. Ribbons of vegetation mark the presence of shoreline hot springs and attract many songbirds, including warblers, sparrows, and grosbeaks. Several birds fish in the river, including belted kingfishers, American dippers, ospreys, and bald eagles.

Viewing Information: Excellent bighorn viewing spring through early fall. Peregrine falcons best viewed in spring and early summer; other birds of prey most visible winter and spring. Lots of spring songbirds, but some birds present year-round. Facilities, information, barrier-free access at NPS and BOR visitor centers. Pay substantial fee for commercial raft trip or contact BOR for public access. HOT SUMMER TEMPERATURES, VERY COLD WATER. SOME RAPIDS. WATER FLOWS CHANGE DAILY.

Directions: SEE MAP.

Site Manager: NPS (702) 293-8906, BOR (702) 293-8367
Size: thirteen miles
Closest Town: Boulder City, five miles

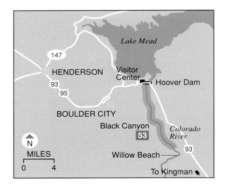

Left: The river trip through Black Canyon brings rafters into undisturbed bighorn country, past several bighorn sheep watering spots along the Colorado River.
GARY KRAMER

Right: The loose folds of skin on this chuckwalla's body are not the result of weight loss, rather a part of its defense system. When threatened, this large lizard runs for a pile of rocks, wedges itself within a crevice, and inflates its body with air.
J.W. WILBURN

54 | VIRGIN RIVER CONFLUENCE

Description: RIVER VIEWING. The Virgin River meanders for miles, empties into a small basin, then funnels through rocky, cliff-lined narrows before it joins Lake Mead. Take a boat northeast from Lake Mead's Overton Beach Marina through the narrows, where rugged cliffs shelter nesting swallows and swifts. Rocky ledges along the way offer fairly reliable views of desert bighorn sheep. Look for chuckwallas on sunny rocks. Enter a compact basin lined with mudflats and marshes—if lake levels are low during peak migration periods, the mudflats teem with shorebirds and wading birds. In the shallows, watch for willets, black-necked stilts, and long-billed curlews; spotted sandpipers, semipalmated plovers, and killdeer will be close to shore. Marshy areas may hide white-faced ibis and, occasionally, flamingoes. Rafts of white pelicans and Canada geese gather in the open water. Clark's, western, and eared grebes are common; California brown pelicans make occasional appearances. Watch the skies for peregrine and prairie falcons.

Viewing Information: Good viewing of bighorn sheep in summer. Outstanding birding year-round, particularly spring. Suggest very slow engine speed, ample distance, and quiet for best viewing. Facilities at marina. BOATING TREACHEROUS WHEN WINDY; SUDDEN WEATHER CHANGES.

Directions: SEE MAP.

Site Manager: NPS (702) 394-4040
Size: Five-mile boat ride
Closest Town: Overton, thirteen miles

55 VALLEY OF FIRE STATE PARK

Description: This ancient sandstone valley, colored in hues from vermillion to gold, features a fantastic array of pinnacles, caves, domes, and arches. Scan the cliffs near the west entrance for desert bighorn sheep. Washes and canyons throughout the park are dotted with creosote bush, brittle bush, and beavertail cactus. Look at the base of these plants for desert iguanas and Gila monsters. Rocky areas are preferred by desert banded geckos, collared lizards, Great Basin whiptails, and chuckwallas. Desert tortoises, sometimes visible in late spring and early fall, burrow in sandy washes and dunes. Golden eagles, turkey vultures, and red-tailed hawks can be seen soaring; ground squirrels and antelope ground squirrels appear everywhere. Equally visible are ravens, roadrunners, sage sparrows, house finches, and several wren species.

Viewing Information: Best time to visit is October through May. Good views of bighorn in fall and winter. Good viewing of predators and small mammals year-round. Birds of prey common in spring and fall. Best reptile viewing spring through fall. Look near visitor center for desert iguanas and chuckwallas. Many trails. Outstanding Indian petroglyphs. Spring wildflowers. Some barrier-free facilities. VERY HOT WEATHER; COME PREPARED.

Directions: SEE MAP.

Site Manager: NDSP (702) 397-2088
Size: 38,000 acres
Closest Town: Overton, ten miles

A member of the cuckoo family, the roadrunner lives on the ground and survives by running from danger and running down prey. Greater roadrunners consume everything from seeds and fruit to insects, lizards, and birds. Their bulky nests are located in thickets or cactus clumps.
JAMES KIRK GARDNER

WHERE TO FIND POPULAR WILDLIFE OF NEVADA

This index lists some of the more popular, uncommon, or unique species found in Nevada, as well as some of the best places to see them. The numbers that follow each species refer to viewing sites in this guide.

LARGE MAMMALS

California bighorn sheep 13, 14, 15
Desert bighorn sheep 52, 53, 55
Mountain goat 23, 24, 25
Mule deer 8, 14, 19, 24, 35, 37, 39, 50
Pronghorn 1, 21, 33
Rocky Mountain bighorn sheep 23, 24, 25
Rocky Mountain elk 21, 34, 35, 43

SMALL MAMMALS

Antelope ground squirrel 46, 52, 55
Beaver 4, 17, 24, 36, 43, 46
Coyote 1, 12, 21, 33, 39
Pika 15, 23, 25

BIRDS OF PREY

Bald eagle 7, 28, 29, 53
Golden eagle 1, 10, 14, 21, 27, 37, 47
Northern goshawk 7, 11, 19, 42, 43, 49
Northern harrier 8, 18, 22, 26, 29, 30, 47

PERCHING BIRDS

Clark's nutcracker 7, 23, 24, 25, 37, 43
Hummingbird 5, 24, 32, 42, 50, 51
Mountain bluebird 1, 11, 17, 32, 43, 50
White-throated swift 2, 17, 31, 40, 52, 53

SHOREBIRDS/WADING BIRDS

American avocet 26, 29, 30, 38, 48, 54
Great blue heron 9, 18, 26, 28, 30, 47
Sandhill crane 22, 26, 30, 45, 47
White pelican 3, 28, 29, 30, 38, 41, 54

UPLAND BIRDS

Himalayan snow cock 24, 25
Rio Grande turkey 28, 38, 49
Sage grouse 1, 11, 21, 43

WATERFOWL

Canada goose   18, 26, 28, 29, 30, 38, 47, 54
Canvasback 26, 30, 47
Common loon 3, 41
Snow goose 29, 41
Western grebe 3, 26, 30, 41, 47, 54

REPTILES

Desert iguana 55
Desert tortoise 52, 55
Western rattlesnake 1, 20, 31, 46, 52

THREATENED AND ENDANGERED FISH

Ash Meadows speckled dace 48
Pahrump Poolfish 51
Pupfish (several subspecies) 48
Railroad Valley Springfish 44

REFERENCES

This list includes more detailed references for information about the wildlife, habitat, and ecosystems of Nevada.

Nevada Department of Wildlife species lists and pamphlets; available at NDOW offices in Elko, Las Vegas, and Reno. *Nevada Raptors* (1985, NDOW Bulletin No. 8) available at Reno office.

Field guides to birds, mammals, fishes, reptiles, wildflowers, geology, etc.; available at bookstores throughout Nevada.

Great Basin Natural History series (includes technical titles on trees, birds, geology, shrubs, and fish), Max C. Fleischmann, University of Nevada Press, Reno, NV 89557.

The Sagebrush Ocean, Steven Trimble, University of Utah, 1989, Salt Lake City, UT.

WHERE THE WILD THINGS ARE

Falcon Press puts wildlife viewing secrets at your fingertips with our high-quality, full color guidebooks—the Watchable Wildlife series. This is the only official series of guides for the National Watchable Wildlife Program: areas featured in the books correspond to official sites across America. And you'll find more than just wildlife. Many sites boast beautiful scenery, interpretive displays, opportunities for hiking, picnics, biking, plus—a little peace and quiet. So pick up one of our Wildlife Viewing Guides today and get close to Mother Nature!

WATCH THIS PARTNERSHIP WORK

The National Watchable Wildlife Program was formed with one goal in mind: get people actively involved in wildlife appreciation and conservation. Defenders of Wildlife has led the way by coordinating this unique multi-agency program and developing a national network of prime wildlife viewing areas.

NOTES

NOTES

NOTES

NOTES

NOTES

NOTES